JACK DUCKWORTH
HOW TO LIVE
THE LIFE OF RILEY

⟨CORONATION ST.⟩

JACK DUCKWORTH
HOW TO LIVE
THE LIFE OF RILEY

JOHN STEVENSON

First published in Great Britain in 1996 by
Virgin Books
an imprint of Virgin Publishing Ltd
332 Ladbroke Grove
London W10 5AH

A catalogue record for this book is available from the British Library.

ISBN 1 85227 681 9

Designed by Blackjacks Limited, London
Colour reproduction by Scanners
Printed by Bath Press, Bath, Great Britain

Contents

Introduction 6

Early Life and Struggles 8

How to Pull 12

Work and Its Avoidance 16

Women: The Basics 22

Lessons Out of School 25

Getting Plenty of Free Ale 29

Football Crazy 34

How to Be a Great Lover 40

Royal Relations 44

The Pop Star Blues 50

The Older Woman 58

This Sporting Life 62

Contacts 67

Patriotism 69

Posh Birds and How to Trap Them 71

Health 76

Survival Techniques 82

Dangerous Women 86

My Friend Frank Sinatra 92

Man's Best Friend 96

Abroad 102

What's It All About 107

Vera 109

Regrets 112

Introduction

As I stand behind the bar of MY pub – oh yes, granted over the door it says Vera Duckworth is the licensee, but that is just a useful fiction dreamed up by my accountant – I look back over my success story and can honestly say I have lived a life that's full. I have travelled each and every highway.

Life is like an ice lolly. It does not last for ever. The thing to do is seize hold of it and give it big licks before it melts away.

I have many admirers. They prop up my bar, sup their pints, and say: "By hell, Jack, I don't know how you've managed it, but you have done all right for yourself."

True. But if I had known as a young man what I know now, I could have done even better. I sometimes think that if I'd had the help of ten good men (with their own transport) I could have conquered the world.

In this book I explain to you how to go about GETTING PLENTY. Plenty of ale, plenty of crumpet, plenty of this, that and the other. Especially the other.

And you can learn from my mistakes – oh yes, I made mistakes, and I say that not in a shy way. The biggest mistake of the lot ...well, let us just say her initials are V.D. and she is about as much fun.

The record shows I took the blows. But you, my readers, start with a big advantage. You have avoided getting lumbered with Vera. I show you how to build on your good fortune.

Keep this book away from women. If they read it they will learn things they are better not knowing. Knowledge only upsets and confuses women, and they are better off without it.

I have no worries about Vera reading this, since there are just three things she ever reads. Her star forecast. Her catalogue. And her weekly magazine, "Woman's Choice". So, in case you are wondering, there is no danger of her seeing this.

Early Life and Struggles

I have never had it easy, even when I was a kid. In fact, even before I arrived I had a tough time. My mum used to look at me many a time while I was eating a sugar butty and tell me that she nearly lost me twice while she was carrying me.

No, she would say, think yourself lucky you are here, because, believe me, it was not for the want of trying.

The day I was born everybody thought I was a gonner. I was born at home, with my Auntie Matty seeing to my mother. My dad rolled home from the pub with a bottle of pale ale (a sweetener for my mother) just after I arrived. Auntie Matty said I could not live – too puny.

My dear old dad, without a thought for himself, took the top off the bottle of pale ale and pressed it to my feeble lips. The rest is history. And to this day I cannot say no when offered a bottle of pale ale, if only for sentimental reasons.

My Auntie Matty hated to be proved wrong about anything and had a grudge against me for living despite her predictions. She looked like a bundle of washing my Auntie Matty and was a rough old bag. But underneath she had a heart of gold and all the neighbours used to send for her if there was an emergency, like kittens that needed drowning or some old gaffer at death's door – and Auntie Matty would always come along and pull them through.

Auntie Matty at my dear father's funeral. She was always first up after the boiled ham had been seen off.

She also had very fast hands. One of her favourite pastimes was catching flies as they zoomed past her in our back kitchen – God knows there was no shortage of them – and during the war when raisins were impossible to get we were the only kids down our street who ever had any Garibaldi biscuits (home made).

My dad, Harry Duckworth, had a double career. He was a rag and bone man – many's the treat he brought us home from the council tip – and also a bookie's runner. No doubt it is from him I get my love of horses. These things are bred in you. Look at Princess Anne.

Mam. Being able to get her legs up over her head made her very popular with our brave fighting men during the war.

My mam, Maggie Duckworth, was a barmaid. You see, here's me – racing, public houses. Oh yes, as I often say, it is all in our jeans, or trousers as we had in them days (when times were good).

There was never any money to throw about in our house. The only stuff I remember seeing thrown about in our house was the odd saucepan, rolling pin, and one time on my dad's birthday when I can only assume it was a celebration, Mam got him at close range with a tin of peas.

But he was one of nature's gentlemen was my old dad. For instance, he would always go out into the back yard to break wind – if we had company. Unless, of course, the company was from Mam's side of the family who he did not get on with. In their case he would come in from the back yard to break wind.

He had a few golden rules, my old dad, which he passed on to me. A gentleman always takes his cap off before hitting a lady – that was one of his.

I was the youngest kid – or as my mam would laughingly put it, her last blunder – and the older ones used to put on me something shocking. My brother Clifford used me like a human guinea pig. "Come here, our Jack," he would say when him and his pals was stretching a plank across the brook to make a bridge, "come and test this out for us."

This was how I learned to swim.

Or – "Come here, our Jack, you're small enough to wriggle through this window." That time a bulldog got me. The lesson I learned there was to avoid getting stuck halfway through a window, especially with your arse on the bulldog's side.

I am not a religious man, but I cannot help thinking it was God's judgement on our Cliff that the holiday accident insurance he took out came to me – me, not our Vera, though to hear her talk you would not think it – and got me the Rovers Return.

My sister Daisy was no better. On one of his rag and bone expeditions, my dad picked up this old pushchair. I was the first and last in our family to get wheels this early in life – worse luck. Because Mam used to make Daisy take me out in it.

Many's the time our Daisy and her ragged-arse pals used to push me up this hill where the bandstand was in our local park. Having got to the top they would then give the pram a shove and I would find myself rolling downhill into the park lake.

One bonfire night – you wil find it hard to believe this fiendish example of woman's inhumanity to man – she lit a banger and STUFFED IT DOWN INSIDE MY WELLIE.

Dear old Dad, snapped in one of the many pubs he frequented daily, helping to fight the slump by keeping their trade up. He preferred small barmaids as he reckoned they made the pints seem bigger.

This kind of thing would have warped many a young lad. I sometimes find it amazing that in my maturity, as I approach my prime, I am still the sunny-natured, deeply lovable bloke that keeps the punters rolling in the Rovers.

But to this day I sometimes wake up in the middle of the night dreaming I am strapped in a pushchair rolling down that hill towards the park lake – or struggling to pull my wellie off before the dreaded explosion.

Over the years Vera has many a time got the benefit of me waking up in the night like this. In fact, in our house, the phrase "Any chance of getting your wellie off?" became a coded way of referring to hanky panky.

Only the other night the cheeky cow had the nerve to shake me awake and ask me, and I was forced to tell her that the resemblance between one old boot and another was getting closer all the time.

I had other early lessons about women and the villainy they are capable of. At Mixed Infants, Doreen Nuttall took me behind the coke pile and suggested she would show me hers if I showed her mine. Like a fool I agreed to go first, after which she ran away – laughing. Not only that, she only went and told Miss then, didn't she? Said it was all my idea.

Never trust women. They will get you into trouble. The only safe policy is – get them into trouble first.

With my brother Clifford. Usually it was me who carried the can.

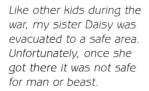

Like other kids during the war, my sister Daisy was evacuated to a safe area. Unfortunately, once she got there it was not safe for man or beast.

How to Pull

A woman you can fancy is like a good pint of ale. You want one that is full-bodied with a good top on it. One that goes down nicely.

And, also like a good pint, a woman needs pulling. Steadily, with a smooth action. You don't need big muscles. What you need is what I, luckily, have always had bags of – style, charm and confidence.

If you don't ask, you don't get. It is no good waiting for women to make the first move. A pal of mine, with a great track record, believes in the direct approach. No messing. Straight in.

"Hello, love," he says to any passing bird he takes a fancy to. "Do you fancy doing a turn?"

He varies it slightly. He has to go to London a lot (poor sod, the ale's so bad he's glad when it gets to closing time) and when in the Cockney capital he will employ a bit of patter such as, "How am I fixed for a quick Donald?" since the local lasses like a bit of rhyming slang.

Now I will admit that this pal of mine runs into a fair number of rebuffs in the course of a day. He also gets the occasional glancing blow from a weighted handbag or sharp tap with a stiletto heel, but you would be amazed how much positive response he gets. He gets plenty. In fact, he has often told me that if he was getting any more, he would have to take a lad on to help him out.

Me? I go for the more subtle approach. The witty quip that tells a bird she is dealing with a suave man of the world. One chat-up line that has been brilliant for me over the years goes as follows:

"Excuse me love, but don't mind me asking – have you got a cold?"
Now the beauty of this line is that ...

you are well away whatever answer they give you.

If they say yes then quick as a flash you riposte:
"I thought as much. Because you are looking very chesty."
If they say no, you are into Plan B. I give my cheeky little twinkle and:
"I am surprised to hear that, flower, because you are looking very chesty."

Clever, eh? Of course, when I say you are well away whatever answer they give you, I am not counting the occasional mentally retarded bint

Tina Fowler. I gave this girl every chance, but she blew it.

Some women have to be repeatedly shown what is required of them. They seem unable or unwilling to grasp it.

who says something like: "Drop dead grotbag." Let's face it, there are some women who just can't keep their end up when it comes to sophisticated chat.

Another good pulling line of mine used to be: "Hello, darling, where have you been all my life?" A couple of times lately, however, I have run into the dreaded conversation contra-flow with this. The first time, this obviously unbalanced woman said, "I wasn't even born for the first 40 years of it, Grandad."

It was my own fault because she was drinking pints – always a bad sign – and wearing cord trousers. I should have known better.

The second time I used it on this older piece and she proceeded to give me a blow-by-blow account, starting with her childhood on an Accrington pig farm, carrying on to a career as a spot welder in a boiler factory and finishing up with a no-holds-barred account of the various parts of her innards that had been snipped out by surgeons over the last ten years.

I was sorry I'd asked.

Apart from the chat, some blokes swear by the practice of giving women bunches of flowers.

This has never been my way. Partly because I have never lived where there was a park or a cemetery to hand and partly because giving a woman the impression that you are prepared to lay out money on her sets completely the wrong tone for the relationship in my opinion.

I grant you that a certain amount of dosh is necessary for pulling these days when there is hardly a shop doorway you can set foot in without setting off a burglar alarm. You need wheels. A car with a comfy back seat is as good as the honeymoon suite at the Weatherfield Plaza Hotel – and not much smaller by all accounts.

Money helps. Even as a little kid I noticed it was the big lads from rich homes, the ones with a hoop and a stick and a bag of aniseed balls, who pulled in the playground.

One last word, especially for the bashful or the timid. There is nothing women like more than being fancied, so you are in with a chance if you make it dead obvious that you strongly fancy doing them a favour.

When I say make it obvious, this does not mean walking around naked under a long raincoat with no buttons. Do what the smart flashers do in bitter weather – tell them about it. It is always better described than displayed. — *In his case, definitely!! — Vera*

Telling Bet my plan for getting her picture on Page 3. All she had to do was supply the camera.

Work and its Avoidance

It was one of them days you never forget. I was not far off leaving school. Then one evening, my dear old father kept studying me as I sat by the fire combing my rabbit.

He was in an unusually observant frame of mind at the time. There was a brewery strike on round our way,

At your place of work it is never too soon to establish that you suffer from a glass back. Here we see:

a *the quiet but noticeable wince followed by . . .*

b *. . . the brave attempt to ease the agony.*

the pubs had no ale and my dad was noticing things for the first time. Things that normally he took in his stagger.

"Hey up, Mother," he said. "How long's our Jack been in long trousers?"

"Ages, you barmpot," she affectionately replied. "He's leaving school next week."

And then my mother said: "He'll have to go to work."

She had a cruel tongue when she wanted, my mother.

But my dear old father, a wise man, said something to me then that I have never forgotten. "Jack, lad," he said, "I'll give you a bit of advice now.

c *"I think the pain might pass in a minute, boss."*

d *"No, damn it, it's locked. That's me finished for the day."*

Don't you bother your head too much about work. There'll be plenty of it still left when you are dead and gone."

Sound advice. And I have always done my best to follow it. After all, what has mankind been put on this earth for? It is not to drudge and slave all their lives, is it? No, that is what women are here for.

Granted, there are blokes in this world who seem to like work. I have no quarrel with them. If that is what turns them on, so be it, and in this day and age, when there are not enough jobs to go around, my view has always been –

Let those who like it get on with it.

Same with women. I have never been selfish with Vera. I have never held her back, never interfered with her career. In fact, I have always encouraged her to go out into the working world and carve out a full, satisfying life as a rounded human being.

Why should she be stuck at home all day? A prisoner in her own home? I think that's all wrong. Apart from that, women get under your feet when you are sat with the racing page trying to work out the day's investments. You cannot think straight if some woman is blundering about with the vac and asking silly questions like, "Are you going to sit there all day, you great idle lump?"

"Listen, Jack, if I'd spent as much time on my back as you have, I'd be a rich woman."

I have always been a big support to Vera in her career. It was me got her the job at the bottling plant after we got married. It was me that made them keep her job for her after she'd had our Terry. It was me that gave her the confidence later to go for a job on the sewing machines in Mike Baldwin's denim factory.

"Course you can do it, Vera," I said. "You're not a complete idiot, whatever people might say about you."

It was me that persuaded Curly Watts to take her on at Bettabuy. And I warned her time and time again she was stuffing too many tins in her handbag at hometime – but she wouldn't be told.

I have always been the responsible one in our marriage. Without me to buck her up every time she has been fired she would just sit at home, moaning and going to pieces generally.

I have always been good at motivating her (not bringing any money home for her always works eventually) and getting her back to work is good for her self respect – I have helped her to see that being a parasite and sponging off me would completely destroy her self esteem.

In that respect our marriage has been a good partnership. Me the brains, Vera the brawn. And there are parts of my brain that I have not got round to using yet when it comes to thinking of jobs for Vera.

I can honeslty say that I have never been afraid of hard work myself – mainly because I steer well clear of it. Sooner or later, however, the curse of Adams falls on all of us. Work, the curse of the drinking man, gets us cornered. It has been Vera's fault mainly. She has always been awkward about tipping her wages up, so I have been forced to work just to scrape together the bare necessities of life – the price of a few pints and a modest wager or two at the bookies.

Despite this I have never lost my self respect.

Whether I was at the beck and call of a big employer or a small employer I WAS ALWAYS WORKING FOR ME, NOT THEM. There is a lesson for us all. Whether you be a brain surgeon or a shifter of blockages in toilets, a brain prodder or a drain rodder, MAKE THE JOB WORK FOR YOU.

In my experience every job has its perks, or there are things lying about the workplace that come in useful at home. I must admit, though, I have often wondered what there might be worth nicking from, say, the sewage farm. But I would bet money there is something.

Decisions, decisions.
Each way or on the nose?

Talking of sewage farms, my first job was at the other end of that particular chain. Dad wanted me to become a rag and bone executive alongside him, but my mother took advantage of the brewery strike ending and him being suddenly taken drunk one morning. She dragged me down to the factory where they made toilet rolls.

I soon showed my aptitude and before long I was smuggling home up to 80 or 90 toilet rolls a week. Dad was not impressed, mind you. He was a newspaper man all his life, same as Lord Beaverbrook or Rupert Murdoch. Not that he ever wasted good money on buying a newspaper. First he would bring home his fish and chips in it. Next morning he would take it down the yard and read it. Then he would use it.

When Alec Gilroy smiles, you're in trouble. That smile – like moonlight glinting on the the brass plate of a coffin lid.

He was ahead of his time in many ways, my old dad. Nowadays they call that sort of thing recycling.

The bigger the organisation the more use a piece of paper can be. It has to be a big place in my experience – if it is small enough for everybody to know everybody else, this tip does not work.

What you do is you walk about the place, frowning and carrying a piece of paper which you consult from time to time. If you can fasten your piece of paper to a clipboard, so much the better. Don't forget the frown. You will not be approached. Most people suspect they're about to get the chop any day now. They will take you for Head Office's hired assassin, and keep their heads down.

While you stroll about they will work harder. So we see that one talented idler can be useful to the employer.

Be that one man.

I have done all sorts of jobs in my time. A lot of driving jobs, first on lorries, then the cabbing. At one time I also ran my own external glazing services company.

Window cleaner, that's what this means!

— Vera

But all the time fate was leading my footsteps nearer and nearer to my heart's desire – a job in a pub. Getting to be cellarman at the Rovers Return was the summit of my career as a worker. It was like letting a kid into a boiled sweet factory.

Working with Bet Lynch was not easy, though. And Alec Gilroy was even worse. Talk about mean! That man would not give a starving dog the skin off his kipper. With people like Alec, it is important to look busy. This means that you have to make the right noises. Keep saying things like "It's all go round here." When they ask you to do some job or other always say: "Stick a brush handle up my backside and then I can sweep the floor at the same time!"

An employer likes to think that his workers are hard pressed.

Never make a job look easy. Never be too happy. An employer likes you to sweat and suffer for your money.

Wherever you happen to work, establish a personal refuge. Mine was the cellar. I had most of the necessities of life down there. A little wireless, my own darts board and , for self-improvement in that leisured moment, some adult reading matter.

Adult reading! That's what he calls his dirty books! ~ Vera

I made a point of mentioning the spiders in the cellar – as big as Yorkshire terriers some of them – to Bet and Alec. They didn't come down too often and when they did they were too busy keeping an eye out for brawny spiders to notice my little comforts.

Unfortunately, however successfully you manage your employers, sooner or later they will try to push you too far. This is when you will be glad that you have taken pains to establish your handicap. I don't mean Vera. I mean my other handicap – my bad back. Certain malicious individuals, not mentioning no names but her initials are VD, have put it about that I got my back injury when I was thrown out of a public house in Oldham.

This is a wicked lie. If you want to know the truth, my spine was damaged when I was *TRYING TO GET BACK IN.*

I struggle gamely on with it – as I have often told Vera, women do not know the meaning of the word pain – but now and again my body tells me that I need rest and fresh air. A day at the races or, failing that, an afternoon in the betting shop.

Now, here I am, master of my own pub. People work for me. What a turnaround, eh? All my years of working for hard-faced employers have given me insight, warmth and understanding.

My staff know that if they try any of the dodges I have recommended here, their feet will not touch the floor.

Behind the pumps and happy as a pig in muck. Happier some days. Muckier, too.

Women: The Basics

I have heard it said – by clever dicks – that the ideal woman is an alcoholic nymphomaniac who lives over a pub. To that I say – cobblers. (And incidentally mine is as clever as anybody's.)

I happen to be married to an alcoholic nymphomaniac who lives over a pub, so I know what I am talking about.

Man is intended to put himself about a bit. One of the saddest realisations that a young man has to come to terms with is that moment when it finally comes home to him that there are too many birds out there for him to be able to get round them all.

It is a sad thought, and a wave of sympathy goes out from me to all those ladies out there who will never have the luck to experience a little touch of Jack Duckworth in the night.

A man is like a bee; he is programmed to flit from flower to flower, getting a bit here, a bit there. There are many beautiful flowers. The bee that had to spend forty years buzzing round and about the same dishevelled old dandelion would get fed up. So it is with us men.

We cannot help it. It is in our jeans. At the end of a good night out, you drop in the chip shop with your pal. Your pal goes for spam fritter, chips and peas. You yourself go for cod in batter plus the old scollops. When you get outside in the cold night air, you look at his, he looks at yours, and you both end up fancying what the other has got.

So it is with marriage.

All right, I hear you asking yourselves, if Jack Duckworth is so smart, how come he got stuck with Vera, who is as dishevelled an old dandelion as you could meet in a long day's ramble?

Good point, good point. The answer is that we are manipulated by forces outside ourselves. To give you a for instance, here is a little parable.

I keep racing pigeons. Now, the day before one of my cock birds is about to race, I will introduce a strange new male bird to the loft. Next day my racer will fly home as fast as his wings can flap to cut out any hanky panky that might be going on behind his back.

That is my trick with a pigeon. Man is designed to trick birds and in the very same manner, Mother Nature – the old bag – tricks men.

The power that I was manipulated by outside myself was Vera's father. He caught us at it in his garden shed. (I thought at the time – does she <u>have</u> to make all this noise?) A bit later on, when she tells me she is in the club, he comes round to see me with his trusty sledgehammer and a couple of his big tough pals and gives me Vera's hand in marriage. Just

Yes, I know it's in her name. Dogs used to have a licence, too – ask yourself who was in charge of them, though.

her hand would not have been so bad. Trouble is, I had to have the rest of her as well.

So we got wed – and our Terry was not born FOR ANOTHER SIX YEARS. A phantom pregnancy – that was what Vera called it. It was not what I called it.

Yes, Mother Nature intends us to be married, and yet there is a bright side to this. The man who avoids marriage all his life has succeeded <u>too well</u>. The married man who plays his cards right can have all the single man gets. He can also have a quiet night in when there is football on the telly. He can get his washing done and his shirt ironed.

Granted, marriage is a mistake, but a mistake it is necessary to make. Without pain there is no pleasure. Young men find this hard to understand, but the passing of the years brings great wisdom.

Looked at positively, marriage is your ticket to a wife-swapping party.

The phantom of the garden shed in between his proud parents.

Lessons Out of School

The day I left school the headmaster – Mr Woodcock his name was, though we called him Old Timbertool – seized hold of my left earlobe and said, "Duckworth, the years you have spent here have wasted my time and the tax payer's money. You are leaving exactly as pig ignorant as the day you arrived."

I was never one of his favourites. But, fair play, he did write a testimonial for me, like to show people when I was trying to get a job. He wrote "Any employer who gets this lad to work for him will be extremely lucky."

I thought that was very nice of him.

But I have to say he was wrong in thinking I'd learned nothing during my school days.

Granted, I was never a teacher's pet in the classroom. Outside the class I used to try to build my muscles up with this system called "dynamic tension". Inside the school I was mostly using a system called "dynamic inattention".

I never learned much geography for instance. In fact, I was so bad at geography the teachers were surprised I managed to find my way to school in the first place.

And I have to admit I got zero marks in the history exam, but then I think I was away the day they did history. And anyway, all the questions in the exam were about things that happened before I was even born.

But I did learn some lessons that have stood me in good stead over the years as I have rambled about in the great playground we call life.

I used to get picked on something shocking. Big lads used to take against me for some reason. They were always bashing me.

Anyway, one night I'm having a quiet sob into my beans on toast, and me mam says, "What are you snivelling for now, you whinging article?"

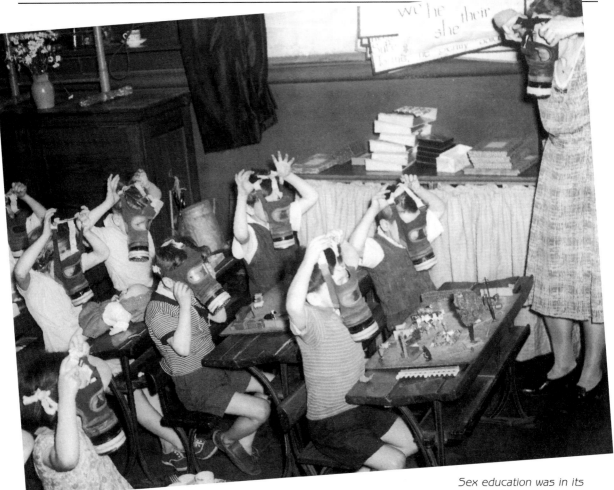

Sex education was in its infancy. We were shown how to pull rubber devices over our <u>heads</u>.

I always think there is nothing like a mother's comfort.

So I told her. And my mam – I'll never forget it – explained what I could do to help myself, emphasising her words of wisdom with a smack on the back of my head in between each thoughtful word.

"You have to make them laugh," she told me. "Laughter," she said, "is what will get them on your side. Amuse them. Laugh and the world laughs with you."

What could I lose? I tried her advice. I made up rude poems about the teachers. I thought up jokes to tell the lads. I did a ventriloquist act with my pet hamster. And it worked. I was the star of the playground. I had the other lads in stitches. Laugh? I had them falling about.

And then, when they'd finished laughing, they bashed me.

Beggar this for a bag of Allsorts, I thought. This 'make 'em laugh' scheme does not work. So I tried singing to them instead. All playtime I sang my little heart out.

As soon as I started singing the bullies cleared off. Well, everybody cleared off. I learned that day – if you can sing the way I sing, the world steps back to make a space for you.

Another lesson I learned was about friendship. My two best pals at school were Dick Williams and Freddie Cartwright. And one year the Olympic Games were on and we all got dead keen on breaking sporting barriers.

So one dinnertime we're in the boys' lavvies out in the yard – all trying for the urine altitude record. And old Timbertool happens to be walking through the yard just when I established a personal best and went well clear over the toilet wall.

"Who did that?" shouted old Timbertool. And quick as a flash my two best pals shouted back, "Sir, it was John Duckworth, sir!"

My two best pals. Who can you trust eh?

Both of them lads left school in disgrace, mind you. Dick Williams was dead good at practical biology. He got the teacher pregnant. Whereas Freddie Cartwright – he was different again.

He got expelled for persistently aiming too low at the leapfrog.

I tell you this. That school never taught me any maths, although I am brilliant at money sums, brilliant. It was my dear old father who taught me that. With him being a bookie's runner on the side I used to carry many a betting slip for him.

When Uncle Bert died, Aunty Ethel gave me his glass eye. But I had no more luck with it than he did.

There was nobody to touch me for working out what a punter stood to win from his crossed doubles, each-way trebles, and a Yankee on the first four at Haydock. And this is old money I'm talking about, proper money, twelve pence in the shilling and twenty shillings in the pound.

I tell you this. Nobody in the Rovers ever gets wrong change off me. Not accidentally anyroad.

And then again, when my dad brought an old dartboard home from the tip and hung it on the kitchen door that was good for my maths training too. That was how I came to be able to count backwards from 301. Come to that it was also how my mam eventually got her ears pierced.

The vulture – easy meat for a big rough bird.

It was my dear old dad who taught me a great lesson one Christmas Day, the first Christmas we ever had a turkey in our house. Me and the other kids are sat round the table, tongues hanging out, and my dad has the carving knife at the ready.

"Now you kids," says my dad. "You can have a choice. A nice helping of turkey or a shiny new sixpence. And, to help you make your minds up, remember there'll be plenty of Christmas pudding to follow."

So we all thought, right, well, if there's plenty of pudding we'll have the sixpence. So we sat there drooling while me mam and dad saw the turkey off. And then my mam brought the pudding in and my Dad said, "Right. Now who would like sixpence worth of this lovely pudding?"

It taught me a lot did that. I appreciate the value of money, I appreciate the cost of food. This is why I never take Vera dining out at these swanky restaurants where they charge you a bomb.

And it is just as well because Vera eats like a vulture.

I only wish the resemblance ended there.

Getting Plenty of Free Ale

*S*trictly speaking there is no such thing as a bad pint of beer. I have supped ale in London pubs which, to me, tastes of gnats' pee or as pale and paltry as a maid's water. Yet, standing next to me at the bar are Cockneys hurling it down their necks with every sign of enjoyment. It all comes down to what you are used to. This does not stop the punters arguing. Many a time in the Rovers I stand listening to my customers arguing over the merits of ale. Sooner or later they turn to me and say: "Jack lad, you are the expert, which is the King of Beers?"

I give them a quiet smile and reply: "The King of Beers, lads, is also the Beer of Kings, the finest pint you will ever drink" – by now they are hanging on my words – "the best ale in the world is …

the pint that somebody else has paid for."

Here now are the Jack Duckworth tips on how you may stagger through life and public houses supping more than you spend.

In all fairness, I had better offer a Government Health Warning here. In the hands of novices the methods I am about to outline can lead to trouble. In the early years of applying my methods you may well get the odd tongue-lashing. In extreme cases you might come in for a boot up the old backside. If so, bear in mind that practise makes perfect. Do not be discouraged.

ENTERING THE PUB

Do not blunder straight in. Linger on the threshold savouring the mingled aroma of hops, malt, barmaid and gents. While you inhale, scan the situation. Aha! There at the bar is somebody you know buying a drink.

My left hand is in Vera's bag.

☞ TIME YOUR RUN

Do not arrive too early. Make sure your target is being attended to. Do not arrive too late – i.e. when he has already handed over his money. When the moment is ripe, while your man is ordering, approach him from the blind side. His first inkling of your presence should be your friendly hand clapping his back and your friendly voice saying: "Tommy lad! Long time no see!"

If this does not get a reply of "Hello, Jack lad, what are you having?" either you have mistimed it, or you are dealing with a fellow professional.

A word of caution. Make sure you get your target's name right, even if you hardly know him. If you call him Chalky and his name is Nobby, you have run straight into life's offside trap.

Just as important as getting the other bloke to buy you a drink is avoiding having to buy him one back. Bear in mind that a lot of these boozers are drinking far too much for their own good. It is no kindness to them to ladle free ale down their necks. In fact, probably many of them ought to be at work anyway instead of propping up the bar.

☞ THE SUDDEN DEPARTURE

Even as you lift the brimming pint that has just been bought for you, say, in a grudging tone, making the bloke feel that he has detained you against your will:

"I shouldn't be here."

With between two and three inches of your pint left, say, "Well, we'll just have the other half." Immediately glance at your watch and exclaim, "Flaming Nora! Is that the time? I'm in big trouble! It will have to keep, Tommy lad!"

Swallow your two to three inches, clap the bloke on the shoulder saying, "I'll have to love you and leave you," and it's out and away to the next hostelry.

☞ VARY YOUR PATTER

Practise at home in front of a mirror. You should learn the sharp facial wince and hand-to-the-belly clutch of a man with internal trouble.

Look round, say, "Where's the doings?" and, leaving between one and two inches in your glass, head for the Gents. Wait exactly four minutes. You never know, when you return there might be another pint waiting for you. If, on the other hand, all that awaits you on the bar is what you left there, return with an anguished face, nod at your near empty glass, say, "You finish my pint, lads, the old guts are playing up," and head for the door.

Ignore any remarks you might hear along the lines of, "Hey up, here comes the vanishing act."

Some nights you might get tired of having one free pint in a load of different pubs. You might fancy staying put. This is where a whole new branch of the craft comes in . . . .

WHEN TO SUGGEST A KITTY

It's a fine art is this. Only a complete idiot buys a round and then says, "Tell you what, lads, let's have a kitty."

Numbers is what it comes down to. OK, if there are five blokes in the school, let two of them buy a round and then when the third mug summons the barmaid you pipe up, "No, it's not right. We'll have a kitty."

Those who have not bought (who will fancy a kitty) outnumber those who have already bought (who won't) by three to two.

If your school is an even number, box clever. Say there are four of you. Wait till a bloke who has already bought a round goes to the gents.

By the time he comes back you can have the kitty in operation. A practised artist such as myself can even say, as the mug returns fastening his fly, "Come on, Frank, it's no use you dodging in the Gents. We're having a kitty so give us your fiver."

That much brass on the bar surely calls for a round.

FRIENDS OF WEATHERFIELD HOSPITAL

"I know for a fact there was a five pound note in this handbag."

 COPING WITH THE REALLY BIG ROUND

There are times in the boozer's year when you find yourself in a football team-sized round. This calls for special skills. It is not always necessary to get a kitty going. For the next method of supping Freemans you need A RELIABLE FRIEND OR PARTNER.

OK. Let a few rounds be got in. Naturally you have not paid for any of these. Nor has your reliable friend or partner. At the correct moment you step forward saying, "Right, it's my shout."

Your reliable friend or partner says at once, "Give over, Jack. What are you playing at? You got the round in before last."

If some mug does not immediately shout up, "I haven't bought one yet, this is mine," I will plait sawdust.

When operating this system the smart man always has first go. It is easy to go off people and your friend or partner may be due for a short sharp shock.

So, when it comes his turn to step forward saying, "Right, it's my shout," you may want to keep your trap shut. Let the miserable bugger buy a round. The chances are he is one of those miserable sods with short arms and deep pockets. It does these people good to pay their whack now and again.

Football Crazy

There are times in the Rovers, late at night usually, after hours as like as not, when the lads are talking about Man. United, and some bloke will turn to me, and say "Duckworth ... Duckworth ... it rings a bell does that. Wasn't there a Busby Babe by that name?"

It is my proud boast that I have never been one to brag. But when pressed I have to admit – yes, that Busby Babe was me.

But for an unlucky injury at the start of my career it could have been my name on them cups and trophies. But – but – if it hadn't been for that injury I could have been on the plane in the snow at Munich airport.

I have often thought ...

somebody upstairs likes me.

And I do not mean our Vera, even though as we speak she has turned in early and is lying in bed waiting for me to join her. Well, she will have a long wait.

*Too bloody true.
As usual.
– Vera*

When me and Bobby Charlton were first on United's books as young lads it used to be hotly debated about the club – which of us would be the first to pull on an England jersey?

It was Bobby. As things turned out.

But we were inseparable in them days. We practised signing autographs together. Whatever was mine was his and vicky verka. He borrowed my embrocation, I would use his hair cream. I taught him things, like speed on the ball, showed him where he was going wrong – he had a soft shot through leaning back when he struck the ball.

Then one day – that old, old story. Two players going in hard for a fifty-fifty ball.

*Wouldn't give him fifty for either of them!
– Vera*

The club doctor's eyes were wet when he finished examining my groin. My first-class playing days were over. I hung up my boots, cleared out my locker, and gave Bobby my embrocation.

He gave me his Brylcreem because it was already clear he would not need it long enough to get to the end of the jar.

Mind you, I never turned my back on Old Trafford. Whenever I could help them out I would willingly give of my keen footballing brain. Over the years I managed to sort out many a great player who had somehow lost his way.

Nobby Stiles, one of our World Cup heroes in '66, for instance. He was making the same mistake match after match – until I stepped in.

I spotted instantly what was going wrong, and from then on – after my quiet word with him – Nobby used to leave his teeth in the dressing room before trotting out on to the park.

Busby babes boarding the bus.

Getting rid of the excess weight put an extra yard of pace on him. And if any opposing forward heard Nobby's pounding feet and felt his hot breath behind him – when he turned his head, Nobby was still a fearsome sight, even without his teeth.

All right, he might not bite you – but you knew you could well be in for a nasty suck.

I know where he gets these photos faked – Vera

Then again, I remember being in Belfast one weekend – a lads' outing, to do with racing pigeons. And in a park I saw this young lad playing. Back in Manchester I tipped off my old friend Matt, and the rest is history – Georgie Best.

Not many people know that Georgie nearly tore off the red shirt and threw up the game even before he was out of his teens.

A shy, diffident lad, he was never happier than in his bedroom at the digs, doing a 30-piece jigsaw and drinking a mug of hot chocolate. But on the practice ground at United – nothing.

I remember Matt, as he then was, whimpering "I'm sick as a parrot, Jack. Can you sort him out?"

"Leave it with me, Matt, as you now are," I replied. "I will show young Georgie that there is fun to be had here in Manchester, and that he does not have to go home to Belfast every time he fancies a bag of chips."

I took Georgie round the clubs. I explained to him which were the girls – the ones that bulged out at the front. Granted there were some that didn't, but he didn't need to bother with them – and to cut a long story short Georgie took to it like, er, like – well, like a fish comes to mind.

Before long he would not even look at a jigsaw puzzle, unless it was that year's Miss World in the nude, and even then it would have to be no more than sixteeen pieces, maximum. Matt, as he then was, was over the moon.

These days I sometimes get small-minded blokes accusing me of inventing my friendship with Georgie in the old days. One clever dick came in the Rovers the other day. "I was at a sportsman's dinner last night," he said. "George Best was there, making a short speech. I asked him afterwards, any message for Jack Duckworth? He said he'd never heard of you. How do you answer that?"

Well, I just have to say I am deeply sorry to hear that George has lost his memory like this. I'm not saying it's the drink. It could be the women.

To this day I am ready to help United out of the mire. A couple of years ago Alex, as he now is, said to me, "Jock, I've got a problem with the wee French laddie. He can't seem to get the grasp of the lingo, you know?"

I thought this was a bit rich coming from Alex, but I never let on. So they sent Eric to me once a week and I coached him in useful phrases that you have to have to get by in Manchester.

"OK – we admit that one of us is seeing Miss World. Beyond that, no comment."

Phrases like "Not three bad." or, "Fair to Middleton" or, "You must think my name's Arthur" or, "This is for who kisses Betty".

Or sayings like "You can't get a pig to run after an empty bucket" or, "If yon mon had any more mouth he'd have no face left to wash".

Then one time Eric come to me, looking all puzzled and pensive. "Jack, mon ami", he said, "at zee game a spectator he say to me I have to go take a running jump. Quoi? What ees zees running jump?"

So I explained to him what a running jump was. I even drew him diagrams, and then next week he goes to Selhurst Park and – oh dear, oh dear.

I think this is why when I rang up Alex this last time to ask for Cup Final tickets he got the switchboard to keep saying he was out.

Hang on a minute – I hear my readers saying about now – we are supposed to be getting tips on how to lead successful lives. Where is all this harking back taking us?

Good question. Good answer coming up. When you and the lads are rabbitting on in the boozer, you do not want to be a nobody, a man with no tale to tell.

I myself have a glorious life to look back on. Not every man is that lucky. Some of you may have to invent your exploits.

So be it. Be a winner – way back. This will bring you drinks. Women. Respect.

How to be a Great Lover

The publisher has been on to me shouting "More sex, we must have more sex." Vera has been shouting at me like this for years. And if she was offering me money, like the publisher is, I might take more notice.

But I do have many a good tip or wrinkle for the man who lacks my talent for, and experience of, the old how's your father.

Tip number one, and this is important – never have the wife when you wake up in the morning. Even if you might be tempted.

The reason for this is very simple.

You might come across something better in the course of the day.

Looks like it's been a bad day.

And if you do, and you have wasted your strength on the wife, well you could kick yourself. If you had the strength left. Which you won't have.

Of course some men find it easier than others to resist being tempted by the missus first thing in the morning. I have always found it dead easy.

The drink helps.

Now many of these silly women's magazines are always harping on about what they call 'technique' in the bedroom. But the truth is such 'technique' as is needed in the grand old game of hide-the-sausage is a woman's responsibility.

And many of them are no good at it. Take Vera. (And you would be doing me a favour.)

I remember coming home one night feeling full of my clog. I had been at a mate's house watching one of these porno videos. And – by heck it was good stuff – this woman, she kept making moaning noises. The effect on me was totally erratic. It really got me going.

So anyway I am worked up, and who gets the benefit? Vera. I agree, it's not fair. So anyway, Vera's getting the benefit, and I say "Vera – have you ever thought of moaning?"

"Moaning?" she says. "How do you mean?"

"Well," I say, "while we're – you know, at it – I'd like you to moan a bit. Go on. It's not much to ask."

So anyway, she lies there a bit and then she says "Look at the state of this ceiling. It's a disgrace. When are you going to do something about it? You never do a hand's turn round the house."

I don't know what he's on about. The ceiling does want painting.
— Vera

And that is the best Vera can do when it comes to moaning.

Now, as regards the man's technique – the important thing is speed. Speed is the main thing. Nature does not intend us to loiter – to idle about on the job so to speak. Nature wants us to get on with it – and then start looking around for the next lucky lady.

I was not always as fast as I am. But I persevered and practised a lot on my own.

A bloke I know – and who I had respected until then – once staggered me when we were discussing these matters over a pint. He said he had always done his best to prolong it. "Well," I said, "some of us happen to be already well endowed."

Who on earth is he talking about?
— Vera

No, the bloke said, he did not mean like that. What he was talking about was spinning it out. And he said a method he used was to think about something boring while he was at it, and then he did not get too excited.

I admit I did try this once. I was with this nice young bird, and to stop myself getting too excited I thought about Vera – and the upshot was I could not get excited at all. This was naturally very upsetting to me, especially since I had paid for five snowballs and a gin and orange.

So my advice is – beggar this spinning it out for a game of soldiers. It's a mug's game. I grant you, you do come across the odd woman who wants to make a meal of it, but it is bad policy to indulge women's whims anyway.

I have often said, and it is very true, "Give them an inch and pretty soon they want all three."

Don't get me wrong. I have never been afraid to experiment, to try something a bit different.

For instance, there is no law which says the bedroom is the only place you can do it.

It can be a very good idea to do it downstairs on the rug in front of the fire. Especially if there happens to be football on the telly.

I told you. It's all in his head. – Vera

*I'm not being choosy.
I think Vera's looking.*

"I've got a ground sheet in the cellar that's never been tested . . . "

Not difficult!
— Vera

But you get some disappointments, too. I remember as a young man being told by all and sundry that it was great doing it in the bath. But when I tried it I was frankly disappointed. For one thing the coal hurts your knees.

Cars – yes. Certainly. I expect over the years I have had more of that there in cars than I have had at home.

A tip on technique here. The man of the world always puts the car in gear when he parks. I relied on the handbrake once – on a steep pub car park – and ended up rolling slowly into the concert room during amateur talent night.

Still. We did get the 'promising newcomers' award.

One last word. Especially for headstrong young men. If you find yourself with some bird who you have only just met, you know nothing about her, but one thing has led to another – and now you are about to do her a favour – well lads, for your own peace of mind it makes sense to take certain precautions.

I suppose I am going to have to spell this out. OK lads, what I am saying is – don't tell them your real name.

Royal Relations

My wife Vera, the moon of my delight – and believe me when she is getting undressed for bed it is just like a big full moon coming up over the bed end – is the Queen's cousin. That's right. Vera Duckworth and Her Gracious Majesty, Queen Elizabeth the Second – blood relations.

Now how Vera came to discover this is a bit of a long story. All starting when Vera's mam died. This long-time boyfriend of her mam's – Joss Shackleton by name – come up to Vera at the funeral and explained how he was really her dad.

And he was too! Which I could not help thinking was a bit flaming rich. The bloke who caught me at it with Vera in his garden shed, the bloke

"Kids! Nothing but heartache, eh?"

who talked about shotguns and broken legs and made me marry her – he wasn't her father after all!

Talk about life's rich tapestry, eh? You wouldn't chuckle.

So anyway, not only is old Joss Vera's real dad, owing to hanky panky with Vera's mam going back to the year dot – but he is also, he tells her, King Edward the Seventh's grandson.

Not legit, of course. Wrong side of the blanket. But they say hanky panky runs in families, don't they?

The way Joss used to tell it, his granny was a housemaid at some big stately home in Yorkshire where King Eddy – or Prince of Wales as he then was – used to come shooting birds.

And he can't have been firing blanks because after the housemaid's knee took his fancy he went and put her in the pudding club. And the upshot was Joss's mam.

It was all discreetly handled. When Joss's granny's pinny started bulging a bit she was invited to bundle up her bits and pieces and step outside in the snow and start walking. And a bit of money changed hands to make sure she didn't start shouting the odds.

"Too bloody right, chuck."

"If you're Charlie doesn't sort himself out, we'll end up with a republic!"

Years later, when she was about to go to the great back kitchen in the sky, Joss's granny told Joss's mam all about her Royal Daddy.

And in her turn Joss's mam passed it on to him.

And he, when he started feeling a bit doddery himself, broke the news to Vera. Told her how she was Edward the Seventh's great grand-daughter, how the blood of kings ran in her veins.

I remember saying to her "Descended from a King Edward eh? The latest in a long line of potatoes. A chip off the old block you might say."

Vera doesn't like that kind of talk. Takes it very serious, this royal blood bit. Likes looking at photos of old King Edward, and Prince Charles, and herself, and our Terry – and saying "You can see the likeness can't you?"

And as for me, according to Vera, I am just a humble commoner and by rights ought to walk two paces behind her – like you see Prince Philip doing with the Queen.

She sends the Queen a card every Christmas and every birthday – which is two a year don't forget. It all mounts up.

And when old Joss kicked the bucket, Vera started fretting. "The Queen ought to know," she kept saying. "He was family when all's said and done. She'd want to be told Joss has gone."

So the silly old stocking-top writes a letter. "Dear Your Majesty, etc etc," tells her how Joss has snuffed it, how he always spoke well of her, was dead loyal, etc etc. Signs it at the bottom – "Your loyal and obedient cousin, Vera Duckworth (Mrs)".

I offered to post it for her (intending to tear it up and chuck it in the bin) but Vera insisted on dropping it in the box herself.

A few days go by. No reply from the Palace. I expect they get letters from nutters all the time. Vera starts fretting. "They're keeping it from

"You can see the likeness, can't you?"

her," she starts saying. "It's not right. I'll have to go down there myself, in person, and tell her Joss has gone."

Well, I could see this turning out a bit awkward. I thought – I'll have to do something. So I did.

Two mornings later a letter comes to our house. Addressed to Vera. London postmark (we don't get many of them). Nice posh envelope. And inside there's a deepest sympathy card. All hand-written.

To our trusty and well beloved Vera.

Greetings.

We are deeply sorry to hear about Joss,

From all accounts, he was a lovely-natured lad, and will be sadly missed,

We have asked our Poet Laureate Mr Hughes, to knock up a few lines (as is his duty)

So here it comes.

We will always remember.
That evening in July,
The tea was brewed,
The bread was cut,
The fire was banked up high.
He went for the chips,
He never came back.
We often wonder why.
God saw he was tired,
And thought it best,
To take him upstairs,
for a rest.
Saint Peter shouted
Look who's here Boss,
The Pearly Gates opened,
And in walked Joss.
— E R

P.S. Philip sends his best regards to Jack.

Well it made Vera's day. It's kept her quiet ever since. That E.R. by the way, that is my mate Ernie Rogers, who drives a lorry up and down to London, and posted the doings for me as well as helping with the poem.

I have to say Vera's royal chatter gets on my wick a lot of the time. I can be just dropping off to kip and all of a sudden Vera will say, "I'm worried about our Margaret." Or, "Wait till I see that Charles. He wants his legs smacking."

But it does have its uses. Only the other day I happened to have hold of Vera's handbag when she come into the room sudden. I'd picked up her handbag to shift it off the settee so I could sit down like, and it had just come open in my hand – must be a loose clasp or something.

She's got a nasty suspicious mind has Vera, and I could see she was going to go raving mad, so quick as a flash I said, "What about that

He's making this up! It's genuine. It's from her majesty. Vera

then, eh? Charles and Di getting back together again – summat about it on the radio just now."

And she was that excited she forgot all about her handbag.

Vera thinks we're going to get the royal invite one of these days. A summons to tea at Windsor.

Well you never know. I wouldn't mind having a talk to the Queen about her racing pigeons in the Royal loft. We could mate her birds to mine.

It wouldn't be all my advantage, you know. Her pigeons might have a better pedigree, but what mine don't know about dodging cats … I reckon it would be a fair deal.

Yeah, well, now I've remembered Just you wait!
— Vera

Vera's great granny and her prince. It's amazing what a man can fancy when he's had a drink.

The Pop Star Blues

We were talking about the Swinging Sixties in the Rovers the other night and one of these clever dicks who reckon to know what's what – it was Curly Watts now I come to think of it – he said "They say if you can remember the 1960s it proves you weren't there."

I put him straight gently and politely. (As a landlord you have to be courteous to the customers.) "Stop talking through your arse, Curly," I said.

You see, what a lot of people don't know is this. I saw the Swinging Sixties from the inside – because I was a pop idol in them years. I was where it was at. I was with it. —— *He might have been with it then. He's past it now! – Vera*

In fact my career in the pop scene started even sooner, back in the Fifties, sharing a stage with Billy Fury. Yes, when he was just starting out Billy had a backing group. And that was me. Yes – I was a Tantrum.

Billy Fury and the Tantrums. Great act, great sound – because one of us had a great voice. I hate bragging so I won't say who it was.

I taught Billy a load of little tricks. Like that run he used to do, through the audience, finishing with a leap up on to the stage. Remember that?

Me with the groupie from hell.

50

Billy liked me to smoke his joint while holding my own.

He stole that off me. Because he'd seen me do it the other way a time or two – jump down off the stage and run OUT through the audience. Sometimes with the band following me.

But then trouble started between us. All down to jealousy. Billy got dead sulky because of all these young girls hanging about after the show – and screaming when they saw me. He couldn't take it. Me getting all the attention, all the ravers. And so he threw a Tantrum – not me, the other lad – and went solo.

Me? I went solo myself. I worked up this great act, totally different, dead original. I was the singing Cockle Seller.

I used to come into the pub or club where I was booked, wicker basket slung round my neck, selling bags of cockles and shrimps, warbling away. The women went mad for it. Some nights I had more cockle than I could cope with.

Then one night fate was waiting in the wings. I was working in the Pink Atoo club in downtown Haslingden – it was very much the 'in' place in the early sixties. Its proper name was the Pink Cockatoo, but the neon sign had been on the blink for years. Still, like the owner used to say, he could easily have got a worse result.

Ringo denied point blank that it was his turn to go to the chip shop.

Then, the night I'm talking about, this smartly dressed bloke asked for a word with me. "You have a great voice, John" – I was still John in them days, Jack came later on – "but answer me this. It is an important question and I want an honest answer. Can you play the guitar?"

OK, I gave him an honest answer.

"I do not know if I can play the guitar," I said. "I have never tried."

The bloke, Epstein his name was, said, "I appreciate your frankness. To be honest, if you can hold the guitar the right way round that will do to be going on with."

What it come to, this bloke had a little group lined up, at least he had three of them. What he needed was a leader – a lad with hard good looks, a rebel image, a sharp and gutsy style. So he come to me.

He took me over to Liverpool to meet the other three. "John", he said, "I want you to meet Paul, George and Ringo."

They seemed nice enough lads – for Scousers – so I told them I was willing to talk about the scheme over a few drinks.

Mr Epstein whispered in my ear. "We have to watch Paul with the drink", he said. "Once he's had a couple all he wants to do is get pissed and shout."

"Pissed and shout?" I said. "Could be a song there somewhere."

Anyway, the lads begged me to help them out, and helping others has always been my way. So while me and the lads started practising together old Brian got us some suits made with our names on the lapel.

Then one day he says "Lads, I have got you your first booking. Next week The Bootles make their debut."

"The what?" I says. "I'm not being in any fllamin' band called The Bootles. It's naff."

But Paul stamped his foot and said it had to be The Bootles because they all came from near there, and anyway they'd already had it painted on Ringo's drum kit. So I let them get on with it. I walked out.

They got another lad called John – Mr Epstein said he had to be called John because he'd had that name stitched on the suit, and suits didn't grow on trees. They wound up improving the name a bit– like I said they'd better – and pinched a few of my song ideas. I wrote to them more than once pointing out I ought to have a few bob coming to me, and they never even replied.

All right, I admit they did well, I admit they were big. But I cannot help feeling that if I had stuck with them …

they would still be big today.

Mind you, I was glad to be out of Liverpool. The Manchester end of the Mersey is definitely the best. Apart from anything else at our end we can always have a Jimmy Riddle – or even the full Nelson Riddle – into the river and …

there is no way the Scousers can stop it flowing down to their end.

There were some great groups in Manchester in them days. I was Rod Thrust and The Squirmers. I was even Gay Pride and the Pile Drivers – we was innocent then.

I knocked about with all the big names. Freddy and the Dreamers. I knew Freddy when nobody would sleep with him, let alone dream. The Hollies – I knew them when they were still the berries.

They were mad years, wild years. People nowadays often say to me "Come on Jack, admit it, I bet you were on the pot."

Well, okay, yes I was. Because in those days we did not have an inside toilet.

And I admit I experimented with certain substances. There was a white powder that I got hooked on, I could not get enough. Lemon kaylie it was called, they sold it at the corner shop years before Alf Roberts had it.

But in my pop years the most foolhardy thing I ever did was to stand next to Shakin' Stevens in the gents urinal.

"For the last time, Stanley, there is no money in singing."

In the end I moved away from the groups, and into singing with the big bands, singing standards, Britain's answer to Frank Sinatra. But that is another story.

I kept an interest in pop though, and I helped a couple of young lads to make it big. There was Len Fairclough's lad, young Stanley Fairclough.

He changed his name to Peter Noone, and did well as Herman and the Hermits.

And old Ena Sharples' grandson, little lad name of Colin Lomax, after I spoke to him he went to the USA, changed his name to Davy Jones, got in the Monkees.

I can truthfully claim to have put both these lads on the right road.

Yes! When they were only kiddies, he told them both to clear off and play in their own street!

"Eeeeee . . . you little Monkee."

The Older Woman

"The older woman?" I hear you saying. "Beggar that for a game of soldiers!" To which I say – hang on, lads, hang on. Take it from me, there comes a time as you stagger down life's ginnel when all of a sudden you will catch yourself fancying some passer-by who must be 50 if she is a day.

Your senior citizens these days come in all shapes and sizes.

I know young men find this hard to credit. But believe me, sooner or later it happens to us all. I even found myself fancying a traffic warden one day last week.

Don't get me wrong. I am not saying you find yourself lusting after weather-beaten old washtubs. I am not troubled by any wicked thoughts when I'm serving old Phyllis Pearce or Maud Grimes ... though, mind you, Maud does have her own wheels which is an attractive quality in a woman.

The fact remains there are some tasty old slappers about. Many of them glad of a bit of notice. I met one the other week in the opticians. I was asking about getting my frames repaired; I mean, I've only had them

The range is enormous –
all the way from your old
scrubber to your vintage
crumpet.

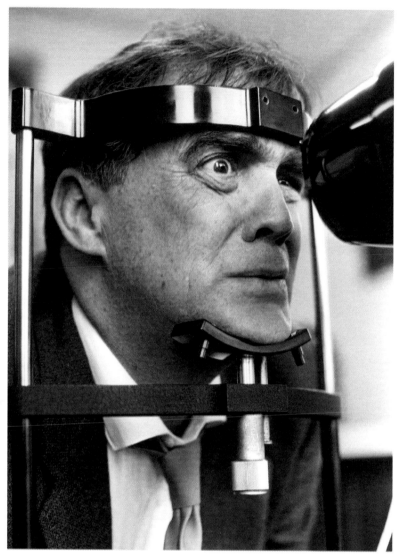

Whoever writes these eye tests cannot spell.

a couple of years, they shouldn't go that fast should they? They was only stood on by a child, not as if it was a grown heavy person. But shops do not know the meaning of the word service these days.

However. This older bird trying on pairs of glasses. I waited while she took her own pair off and then shoved my oar in, very smooth and gallant.

"Excuse me, love," I said. "But when you take your specs off – you look beautiful." She peered at me for a bit and then said "Come to mention it, now I've got my specs off – you don't look too bad yourself."

After that we were away – mention of taking things off had broken the ice – and one thing led to another and the upshot was .... well, they shouldn't put curtains across the cubicles, should they? Anyway, there are plenty of other opticians we can go to.

The good thing about older women is they are inclined to be grateful for a bit of attention. Unlike younger birds, a sulky lot in my experience, the older woman is much more persuadable to get up and get the chip pan going afterwards. Some of 'em will even do you little treats, like a bit of steak, or liver and onions. It all helps you get your strength back.

And the older woman is not likely to have been spoiled and ruined by all these magazines egging them on to demand athletic nonsense. They do not demand hours of this foreplay rubbish. In my view having a drink and a bag of scratchings bought her is all the foreplay a sensible woman could wish for.

Nor do they start shouting "Is that it?" and crying out for seconds.

A sound rule in my experience is …

leave them wanting more.

He can do that all right! – Vera

This Sporting Life

have always had a lot of time for sport, me. Not just football - even though, as I have said, I as a United star in the making and would have ended up playing for England had it not been for that unlucky groin injury.

Jonah Lomu

Round our way is a hotbed of Rugby League and, with me being a well-known sporting landlord, I am a popular figure at the Wetherfield club's famous ground, Wastetippings. (This should not be confused with Oldham's ground, Watersheddings.)

The manager, Errol Swindlehurst, is not only a big pal of mine but a very good customer at the Rovers Return. Errol loves his ale. In fact, if we ran out of glasses he would happily sup it out of a sweaty clog.

In the evenings he is a brilliant manager. In the mornings he is useless.

Now the other week we had a session at the Rovers and I was advising him that if Wetherfield is ever going to get into the Super League we are going to have to buy a big star. From the other lot, the union side of the game, if we have to.

"Go for Jonah Lomu," I said to Errol.

"Brilliant, Jack," he said, "brilliant. This calls for another drink."

Then he wakes up next morning, all befuddled, and sends off a contract to Joanna Lumley.

Joanna Lumley

Master of Hound Bert Latham is attacked by hunt saboteur Mavis Wilton.

We haven't heard back from her yet, but if she decides to accept the contract the silly sod sent her, she has got the club over a barrel. (She could have me over a barrel if she played her cards right.)

Looking on the bright side, if she does pick up the contract, well, OK, she won't be much of a tackler on the field.

But on the other hand she would probably be brilliant in the bath after the game.

None of us. Duckworths have ever gone in much for hunting and shooting. Though my Uncle Frank, who was an engine driver, did plenty of shunting and hooting.

I have hunted the fox. Once. A great big dog fox used to come round Coronation Street, knocking over the dustbins and foraging. And one time it got two of my lovely pigeons, Dolly and Molly.

My pal Bert Latham brought his dog Boomer round and we lay in wait till it had another go. We're out into our back yard like a shot and followed its trail. I meant to shout "Tally Ho" but we'd just had a jar or two so I couldn't just bring it to mind. So anyway I shouted, "After the bleeder."

"Is it you or the dog making that smell?"

And we'd have got the thing and all if silly old Mavis Wilton hadn't come to its rescue in her back garden and bashed poor old Bert over the head with a frying pan.

I did a bit of ratting in Rochdale in my early years. And I remember seeing my Uncle Sid (on my mother's side he was) put a rat down his trousers for a bet one night, and then send his pet ferret down after it.

What happened down there I don't know. But the ferret was never any good after that. And a week later all the rats on our side of the street migrated across the road.

Fishing? No. It's drowning worms as far as I'm concerned.

Athletics? I can watch it on telly. Especially if it's a ladies hurdle race.

Tennis? To me this would be a much more watchable sport, if, at Wimbledon and such like, your really top tournaments, the ladies played without being hampered by them costumes.

My great love is racing. Not so much the dogs, though I had many a happy night at the old Salford dog track, following a betting system that a pal of mine worked out.

Studying form.
The syndicate weighs up
the trainer of Betty's
Hotshot. Nice fetlocks.

He reasoned that any dog seen to drop a load while being taken down to the start would be a happier and lighter beast and should be backed. We were a couple of quid up on this system until the unfortunate outbreak of canine dysentery in 1969.

Horse racing, as proud part owner of Betty's Hotshot, is my greatest thrill. It's a great day at the track when your very own horse is having an outing.

Stood in the paddock with the rich and famous, watching the horse walk round, admiring its glossy coat that it gets from eating its head off.

Asking the trainer why it costs so much. Watching your horse trying to keep up with the others. Listening to the jockey cursing afterwards. There is no thrill like it, believe me.

As it happens, the Rovers syndicate has decided for genuine reasons, health reasons, to put Betty's Hotshot – a horse which has a great future – up for sale. If interested apply to me at the Rovers during licensed hours. No time wasters.

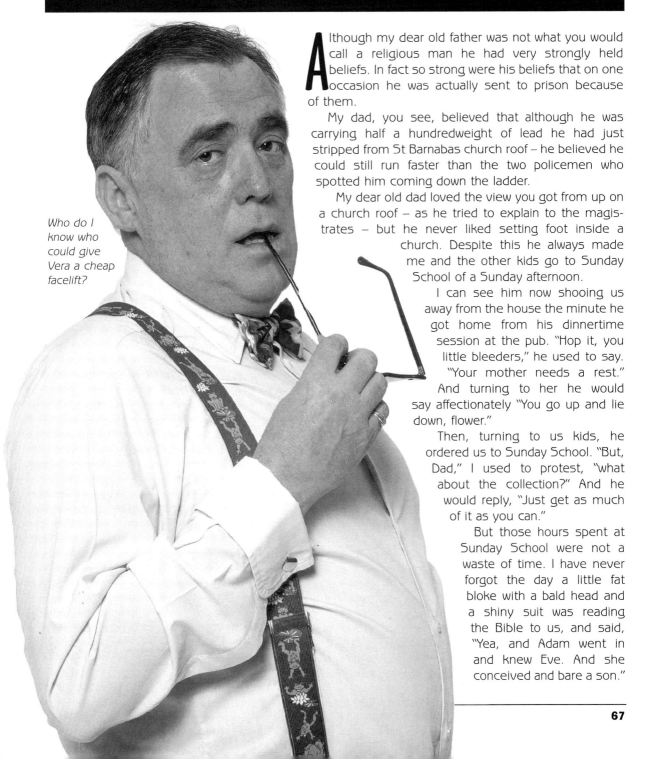

Contacts

Although my dear old father was not what you would call a religious man he had very strongly held beliefs. In fact so strong were his beliefs that on one occasion he was actually sent to prison because of them.

My dad, you see, believed that although he was carrying half a hundredweight of lead he had just stripped from St Barnabas church roof – he believed he could still run faster than the two policemen who spotted him coming down the ladder.

My dear old dad loved the view you got from up on a church roof – as he tried to explain to the magistrates – but he never liked setting foot inside a church. Despite this he always made me and the other kids go to Sunday School of a Sunday afternoon.

Who do I know who could give Vera a cheap facelift?

I can see him now shooing us away from the house the minute he got home from his dinnertime session at the pub. "Hop it, you little bleeders," he used to say. "Your mother needs a rest." And turning to her he would say affectionately "You go up and lie down, flower."

Then, turning to us kids, he ordered us to Sunday School. "But, Dad," I used to protest, "what about the collection?" And he would reply, "Just get as much of it as you can."

But those hours spent at Sunday School were not a waste of time. I have never forgot the day a little fat bloke with a bald head and a shiny suit was reading the Bible to us, and said, "Yea, and Adam went in and knew Eve. And she conceived and bare a son."

At that moment it came to me in a blinding flash. One of life's great lessons.

It is not what you know, it is who you know.

Contacts – these are what enrich our lives. Like this book. I would not be writing it for Richard Branston if I had not been a pal of his dad in the old days at the pickle works.

You never know who might be a brilliant contact one day. And the rich man does not have all the advantages in this field.

After all, when your toilet bowl is cracked and wants replacing, who is your best contact? Lord McAlpine? No! The night watchman at the building site down the road.

Anybody who has been in the Army knows the truth of this. In any barracks, who is the best bloke to pal on with? The C.O.? Give over. The Sergeant Major? Do me a favour. The best pal a man could have is the cookhouse corporal.

I knew the lad's father, the lad's father knew me.

As a popular innkeeper I make many valuable contacts across the bar. Fred Elliott, our local butcher – nothing to look at. In fact he has a face like a well-smacked arse. And one of the baldest heads I have ever come across – to be frank, I've seen better hair on pork.

But despite this Fred is a big spit in the Square Deal. So is Alf Roberts. Both of 'em masters of the funny handshake. And they are going to get me into the local Rectangle. They have told me that if I start at the bottom and work my way up one day I could become the Grand Suppository.

Another useful contact of mine is an accountant. Not your chartered exactly. Not your certified. Turf. But all the same. And when an accountant will say to you things like, "I won't take your money, Jack. You're pissed," how do you put a price on friendship like that?

Fred Elliot gives me fundamentally sound advice.

Patriotism

I was lying in the bath this morning – first Friday in the month, without fail, whether I am dirty or not – like I say, I was lying in the bath this morning, and I could not help thinking to myself, "Yes, we still have one or two things we can be proud of in this great country of ours."

I am a patriot you see. Oh yes. I have done my bit. I have been up at the sharp end defending the country against her foes. Yes, for two years I wore Her Majesty's uniform. Though to be honest I dare say it fitted her a damn sight better than what it fitted me.

In this respect I take after my dear old father. He was a patriot to the last drop of his blood. He always stood to attention when they played 'God Save the Queen' and he insisted other people should do the same.

Unfortunately he had no ear for music. I remember seeing him leap to his feet one time, snatch his hat off and then belabour this bloke in the next seat who refused to stand up.

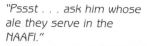

"Pssst . . . ask him whose ale they serve in the NAAFI."

Like I say he had no ear for music. The band was only playing 'Ragtime Cowboy Joe' at the time.

If this man is so clever, why does he keep getting married?

Still, at least my dad's heart was in the right place. Even if his nose was not, after the bloke he belaboured with his cap had finished with him.

My patriotism is based on deep thought and sound reasoning, and the knowledge that in this country we have those things that make life really worth living.

The best ale. The best potato crisps. The best pork scratchings and meat pies. Our Chinese takeaways make other country's Chinese takeaways look silly.

Mushy peas! Show me another country that can offer a mushy pea as good as ours and I will plait sawdust.

All right, people moan about our weather. There's nothing wrong with it. It's always there when you want it, and it stays outside the house. And it's exactly the right length for the football season.

Best of all we are dead lucky being born British, because if we had been born abroad we would all have had to grow up learning a foreign language.

I have pointed this out to Ken Barlow more than once, but despite him being educated and a teacher he does not seem able to grasp it.

Our Vera is even more patriotic than I am. She has a red, white and blue nightie that she wears on special occasions. As soon as I see it on the bed end I know I am in for a replay of "Our Finest Hour". *As if!* *He's doing well at five minutes! - Vera*

Posh Birds & How to Trap Them

I have already laid out a few good tips on pulling women. If you have mastered these things you should now be walking about with a smirk on your features – and perhaps the occasional black eye or cut head.

Now you are ready to tackle a somewhat different specimen – the upper class or intellectual or as we say round here, your actual posh bit of crackling.

A good few of these have come my way over the years. I know what you're thinking. You're thinking "Compared to Vera, they're all posh."

True enough. But I am talking about the really posh who are different from your ordinary bird. For one thing they have more money. This means they are not as grateful when you lavish a couple of snowballs and a bag of chips on them.

Why bother with them then? Because handled right they will lavish the drinks and chips on you.

I was not the first in the Duckworth family to sample the upper crust bird. My granddad Ephraim Duckworth, who for many years was official cat throttler for Bolton Corporation, once confided to me wistfully that, apart from Granny, the one conquest in his life had been a titled lady.

As posh as you can get. Now back in circulation.

She was one of these Suffragettes apparently, a votes for women campaigner, and Granddad met her when she had chained herself to the railings outside the town hall by way of protest.

Granddad often spoke of her. "By the cringe," he used to say, "she were a handsome woman. I'd have liked to have had more of her sort.

But mind you, I don't suppose I'd have got all that far with her if she hadn't been chained to them railings."

In my experience your posh bird, besides being arty crafty, is often riddled with guilt over the plight of the less fortunate. It does you no harm to hark back to childhood and make mention of a little sister with leg-irons or a brother with a bad cough who died the day before the annual choir outing.

I met my first in the art gallery in Manchester. I only popped in there looking for a gents. (I didn't find the gents but there was no shortage of massive sculptures, so it was OK.) There she was, studying a picture of this nude lady. We had a good discussion about it. I mentioned that I had

Grandad often revisited the scene of his happiest moments.

always had a lot of time for well-made busty girls, and it was the start of a beautiful evening.

Art galleries are good places for this kind of bird, but you will be expected to keep your end up. (This is while you are still talking.)

Here is a tip that will get you through the art gallery and as far as the car. (Her car that is.) You can always tell a good painting of a person – they call it a portrait – if the eyes follow you round the room.

Unless it is one by the Dutch bloke, Vincent van thingy. With his, it is the ear that follows you round the room.

In her car, heading for the wine bar – no, it is all right, go with the flow – she will slot a tape into the old cassette player. You will know it is classical music she is playing you, because with this sort of stuff there is no vocal.

"If you find the man, officer, tell him I'm not cross."

Unless it is opera.

Now a lot of blokes get alarmed about opera. No need. Remember that all operas, though they might have different titles, each and every one of them has exactly the same plot.

It is as follows. The tenor wants to give the soprano a good seeing to. But the baritone will not let him.

Bear this in mind and you will be able to have an intelligent chat.

There are many traps for the novice and I admit I have slipped up myself a time or two. Books are tricky. This very well-spoken bird and me were getting on like a house afire until she asked me what I thought of Dickens.

When I told her that unfortunately I had never been to one, she seemed to go off me.

Discussing films can be tricky, too (especially if you are trying to discuss films you have not seen) because the titles can be misleading.

I remember one arty crafty bird asking me if I fancied going to see *Free Willy*. I told her it was fine with me. Well, with a title like that, I was expecting a sex film. It turned out to be about flaming whales.

I would not care except that 30 years previous to this I made exactly the same mistake with a picture called *Moby Dick*.

It is worth making a big effort to hold your own in chat with this kind of bird – because if you can manage it you will not need to hold your own in more intimate dealings that may be on the horizon.

" Free Willy, love? Any time you want to see it . . . "

This type often hangs arond art galleries. A word of warning – they have no money.

Health

The successful landlord of a pub like the Rovers has to be a shrewd judge of men. You meet all sorts. But the kind of customer I have a lot of time for is the chap who looks me straight in the eye and asks me a straight question. The kind of bloke who does not go all round the houses, umming and arring, but comes right out with it and says:

"Jack lad – are you having one with me?"

A bloke who talks to me like that, man to man, is a bloke I can respect. And so when I lift the pint he has just bought me, and salute him, what I say to him is:

"Good health lad."

Not "cheers", not "bottoms up", not "down the hatch", not "all you wish yourself" – no, health is what I wish him. Because your health is everything. Without your health, what have you got? Illness.

This does not mean you have to start taking notice of a load of so-called health experts, or running to the doctor every five minutes.

I never bother going to the doctor if I feel poorly. The only time I go to the surgery is if I want a sick note.

Because what do doctors know about health anyway? They only meet people who are ill. My dear old father had the firm belief that any ailment could be cured by a poultice – or the threat of a poultice. It certainly worked in our house. Once you'd had to put up with one of my Auntie Matty's poultices you'd sooner have died than say you were poorly.

The last thing you want to do is take any notice of these health scares they keep having in the papers.

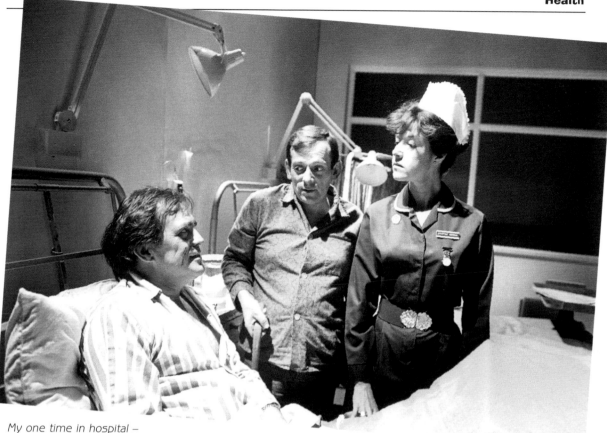

*My one time in hospital –
after falling off my ladder.
The bloke in the next bed
marvelled at my pulling
power with the nurses.*

Mad cow disease? Give over. If I have lived with our Vera for more than 30 years and still not got it – it has to be nothing to worry about.

A bloke I knew, he took all this health rubbish far too serious. He give up drinking, give up smoking, stopped bothering with women, started jogging, lived on a diet to suit a rabbit and never let a chip butty cross his lips. Granted he was healthy, but what was the upshot in the finish?

He died of nothing.

👉 DRINK

There is nothing wrong with drinking. In fact, everything is right with it. Although medical science has proved – and this is sound – that it is far healthier to drink in your local pub than buy stuff at supermarkets and sup it at home.

Drink is good for you, as my dear father proved when he wet my infant lips with his pale ale, giving me my first taste in life. No wonder the ale has always been like mother's milk to me.

People have tried to put me off it and got nowhere. A chap at Sunday School did a demonstration one time – he got this worm, dropped it in a glass of alcohol, and the worm stopped wriggling and died. I remember thinking – fair enough, and it has certainly worked for me because I have never been troubled by worms to this day.

Perhaps if I had, the sport of angling would have had more appeal.

Being a professional, I know practically everything about the beneficial effects of drink, and the best way to go about it.

It is better to drink standing up at the bar.

Not just because you get served faster and the rounds come up quicker, though that is important. But also for health reasons.

Your competent drinker, your man with the hollow legs, needs a straight drop to get the benefit. If he is sat down he is at a disadvantage and the ale builds up at a higher level and makes him feel full.

So, and here is a good tip, it is a good idea to have the WIFE OR GIRLFRIEND DO HER DRINKING SITTING DOWN.

Especially in the early stages, courtship and so on, when having a drink costs double because you are paying for two. No. Sit the lass down. You'll be quids in over the years.

Further to this matter of standing or sitting – drinking while lying horizontal is not healthy. The ale cannot flow properly. Whenever I see a customer of mine lying on the pub floor I make a mental note that he has nearly had enough, and perhaps the time has come for the caring landlord to mind the bloke's wallet for him.

First Friday of every month it's bath time. Stay clean – stay healthy. The spray turned out to be hair lacquer and I couldn't get my arm down by my side all day.

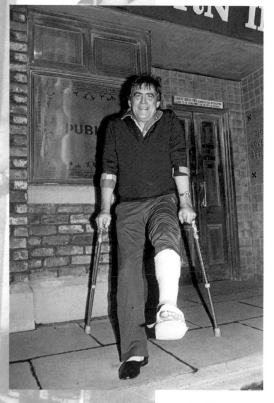

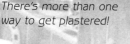

There's more than one way to get plastered!

☞ SMOKING

I will admit straight out that smoking can seriously damage your money. This is why I never offer anybody one of mine. For all I know they may secretly want to give up smoking, so I do not encourage them.

Mind you, if offered one I always accept. Because the person offering may...

subconsciously want to give up.

I help them to get shut of their supply.

And me and Vera have a pact, never to smoke each other's fags. Unless I run out.

They are a hell of a price and you might be better not starting, then you have more to spend on ale. But I've been at it too long to stop now.

The in-place to hang out when I was a kid was the Temperance Bar on Union Street. Old Joe Clegg who ran it used to sell drinks called Stag's Breath, and Dragon's Blood, and Zombies. He didn't smoke himself, in fact he used to say, "If God had meant us to smoke he would have give us a chimney on top of our heads."

But he was always willing to sell a kid a couple of Park Drive, which we all thought was very nice of him.

You would not want your kids to smoke, would you? Well I wouldn't, and I never encouraged our Terry. Because I knew full well he couldn't afford to buy his own and he would forever be cadging or pinching mine.

☞ PASSIVE SMOKING

There is nothing in this. I only wish there was. Because I would not be buying my own. No danger. I would be standing next to the nearest smoker, inhaling deeply.

I have tried this. Not only is there no satisfaction in it, it can also be misunderstood by the touchier kind of smoker. I have had a cut head to prove it.

Anyway, smoking helps me with my ...

☞ EXERCISES

You what? I hear you saying. Jack Duckworth? Exercises. Certainly. Even before I get out of my pit of a morning, I like a work-out. Up, down, up, down – and then the other eyelid.

This kind of exercise is bad for you. Think what Raquelle is doing to their blood pressure!

But once I'm out of bed, this is where the smoking helps me. With the morning cough.

Well, that is how the sparrows round our way start the day, so it must be nature's way.

You need a good heaving cough of a morning to shift the fluids which have settled all wrong during the night. Bound to do aren't they? If you sleep lying down. So once you are on your feet again a good cough helps get the phlegm level adjusted in your lungs. To say nothing of your ears, nose and throat.

Apart from that I get all the exercise I need nature's way. Jogging? Only the horizontal. Bending? I do all that for my shoes. Stretching? I keep my fags on a high shelf.

Stone Age man got his exercise running after rabbits or sneaking up on creatures and eating them before they could wake up. Modern man such as me gets plenty of exercise with a knife and fork.

And a chap hurrying to the betting shop to get his selections on at the last minute is giving healthy use to all the muscles in his body.

☞ PROTECTIVE CLOTHING...

...is the key to sound health. Every November without fail my dear old father got my mam to sew him into his winter vest. The vest did not come off until the following May. If spring was late in Dad's opinion, it could be June.

He was not a great believer in bathing, my dad, in fact he often explained how it washed the natural oils out of the skin. I have not gone completely along with him in this. As I may have mentioned, I have a bath the first Friday of each month, whether I need it or not.

But I have inherited his faith in the vest or singlet. A customer of mine, Arthur Dugdale the gent's outfitter – from who, incidentally, I buy all my vests or singlets – once explained to me how we get the word INVESTMENT from the humble vest. Which just goes to show.

In fact, I wear my singlet not just through the winter, but through the summer as well. My father's patriotic faith in the English climate was his downfall, in my opinion. The fatal chill he caught through lying all night in the gutter outside the Mare and Foal happened in August when he was vestless.

There is a lesson here for us all. Patriotism is not enough. You need a vest as well.

☞ ADULT SECTION.
TO BE READ BY THOSE AGED 18 OR OVER

We all know the tremendous fuss women make about their plumbing. But I have to say, us men go too far the other way. We are too casual with the glorious equipment that nature has given us.

I have always taken the best of care of my flexible friend and its attachments. In my view, if you have tackle to be proud of, as I have, it is worth taking pains to prevent it getting banged, knocked, squeezed, frozen, or – ESPECIALLY – trapped.

My dear old father, brought up on buttons, could never get the hang of the trouser zip. Unfortunately the trouser zip more than once got the hang of him. If you take my meaning. I can still hear his agonised cry.

It's pathetic really.
– Vera

☞ RUDE HEALTH

Not all of us are blessed with this. A pal of mine, Harry Stott, had been having these chest pains. He went to see the quack and afterwards came into the Rovers looking very glum. The doctor had done a load of tests and then told Harry the bad news, which was that he had a dicky heart.

I'm just glad that it is the other way about in my case.

Anyway, back to Harry. The doctor told him that he could have a fatal heart attack at any moment. In future he had to give up drinking, smoking, everything.

He said to Harry, "The slightest excitement could kill you. From now on … no sex either."

Poor Harry. He was crying as he said to me, "I can't drink, I can't smoke, I can't have sex. What am I going to tell the wife?"

I was glad to be able to comfort him a bit. "No, no, Harry lad," I said, "you can still see to the wife. It's excitement you have to avoid."

I'll excite him!
– Vera

Survival Techniques

With any luck there are times in the married man's life when the wife clears off for a bit.

I am not talking about the odd quick trip to visit her mother (in hospital we hope, or better still to put a bunch of flowers on the old bag's last resting place).

No, I'm on about those times when the wife clears off TO TEACH YOU A LESSON. Because she has caught you playing away or otherwise blotting the old shirt lap.

Let the bugger fend for himself – this is how they reason, and their pals egg them on – that will bring him to his senses.

When this happens the bloke who cannot survive the domestic jungle is doomed. I have known pals of mine who ended up begging their wives to come back. Promised them the moon and the stars, even promised to tip up the old wage packet.

These blokes might as well be dead. They are no better than prisoners in their own homes.

It was their own fault. They were all blokes who when the front door slammed, tottered into the kitchen to find a bit of comfort and were instantly flummoxed. The only thing these blokes know how to find is the drying up towel.

You can have a bird in when the wife's away.

Rule number one – know the vital geography. Learn in advance where the wife keeps the bottle opener, the tin opener, the salt, the vinegar, and the sauce bottles. This knowledge can mean the difference between victory and defeat.

I've had to resist the temptation of showing Betty how to make proper hot pot.

Mind you, it is also vital that the wife clears off fondly believing that you are totally hopeless in the kitchen, and doomed to speedy starvation.

So look ahead and act now. Establish yourself securely as a man who CANNOT MANAGE.

Any thinking man will have been doing this instinctively ever since he was married. When the wife asked him to help with the washing up – did he grumble? No. He got stuck in willingly and broke a couple of plates.

They soon stop asking. "Oh give it here", they say. "Get out of the road, go and read the paper or something."

Same when they suggest you make a pot of tea. Make a town halls of it. Give the tea bags a good ripping. Pour the water on it well before it boils.

Never let them realise you can even do a bit of cooking. After I bought the Rovers old Betty Turpin got a bit stroppy and slung her hook. Vera starts faffing and fretting – who's going to make the hotpot?

I could have done it. Dead easy. Did I? You must be joking. Sometimes a man has to crack daft to box clever.

To the thinking husband a good explore of the kitchen now and then, while the wife is out, is a good investment.

You discover all sorts. Like where the wife keeps her savings, the little hiding places she has for stashing the electric money or whatever.

One tip here. Unless the situation is totally desperate never take ALL the money. It's like leaving one egg in a bird's nest seeing as our poor dumb friends cannot count. Same with women.

They reason – well, I say reason, but it's pathetic really – they reason that they must have saved up less than they thought.

Another tip. Make sure you know how to switch the oven on. Don't panic – you're not going to be cooking. Before you set off for the chip shop, you turn the oven on and put a plate in. There is nothing worse than hot chips on a cold plate.

I'll KILL him
– Vera

When you get back from the chippie, open the oven door and – Ah! Ah! you're going to burn your hand. This is where you need an oven glove. Well, this is one thing you will not find because the wife always keeps the oven glove somewhere totally stupid.

Not to worry. Nip upstairs and you'll find some skirt or jumper of the wife's that she has left behind. This makes as good an oven glove as anything.

Survival of a different kind – selling off Clifford's "antiques" to raise a few bob in the bad old days.

Some blokes say the cat makes a good oven glove. I couldn't tell you from personal experience. Us pigeon fanciers don't have cats.

A lot of men are okay for the first week of the wife walking out, but then they begin to crumble. Be strong. All right so the bed is full of crumbs – no doubt about it, this is the one snag about eating pizzas in bed. All right, when it gets really bad sleep at the other end of the bed.

In emergency turn the sheets over. Remember – you are not helpless. Not until the wife comes back anyway.

Practical tip. Mucky feet make sheets dirty faster than anything. It makes sense to do like me – keep your socks on in bed.

Within a few days of the wife clearing off, the downstairs part of the house will have become a complete tip.

Never attempt to clean or tidy up. Never wash a plate or pan.

There are two reasons for this. One, when the wife finally decides to give you one last chance and comes home she will be pleased to find what an impact her departure made. They get real pleasure of knowing you were totally helpless without them. It is cruel to deny them this pleasure.

There's always the chance that an attractive neighbour might want to offer some comfort ...

Two, when your neighbour, old Doris from next door but one, say – or better still, young Doris from next door but one – pops in to see if you have done away with yourself, she will often cluck her tongue at the mess and offer to help you with it.

No, you say, I will not hear of it. No Doris, no, it is not fair on you.

And with a bit of luck, Doris then says – "Well is there anything else I can do for you?"

Well, I'm sure we can think of something can't we? If not, you have not been reading this book with proper attention.

If – and I say IF – you decide you want to get the wife back smartish (well, it's possible, you might need a rest from Doris) all you have to do is get somebody to tip her the wink that Doris has been looking in on you out of the goodness of her heart.

In my experience she'll be back within 24 hours.

I will, I'll kill him.
— Vera

Dangerous Women

Nobody likes women more than me. I have always said that in the right place – and we all know where that is – you cannot do better. But I have to say this. There are women walking about the streets of this country today who by rights ought to be carrying a big placard, on which is written, in big letters: "Government health warning – this woman can get you a cut head, a black eye, and a fat lip."

These women have a nasty gift for getting their men bashed up. I know what I am talking about. I happen to live with one of them.

Take a for instance. Our Terry – who Vera ruined when he was a lad, let him have his own way in everything, she would not be told – our Terry went and put Harry Clayton's daughter Andrea in the club.

OK, there was a bit of bad feeling. I could have coped with that. And Harry Clayton being the local milkman – he's the last one to point the finger isn't he? But then Vera, in the pub one night, has to go and tell Harry and his missus that their Andrea is nothing better than a trollop.

Fighting words. Who gets thumped? Vera? That would have been nice, but no. Terry? No such luck. No, it is yours truly who gets the big wallop.

It cost me a few teeth did that.

See, what it is, women like our Vera – they look round for a war they can start. And then they summon up the fighting soldier – me or some other bloke – and send him out over the top into no man's land.

She did it at Don and Ivy's wedding. Couple of days before I'd had my wedding suit pinched you see. Left it by my seat in this pub in town, went to the gents, when I get back the suit's vanished.

Anyway, at the wedding do, she swears blind she's seen this bloke wearing my suit. Eggs me on, nags me and nags me to sort this bloke out, get to the bottom of it and so on. So I follow this

Sharks go into a feeding frenzy. Women go into a cash frenzy when they find a few quid on you that you didn't ought to have.

They're brilliant our Jack's teeth. They're like stars. They come out at night – Vera

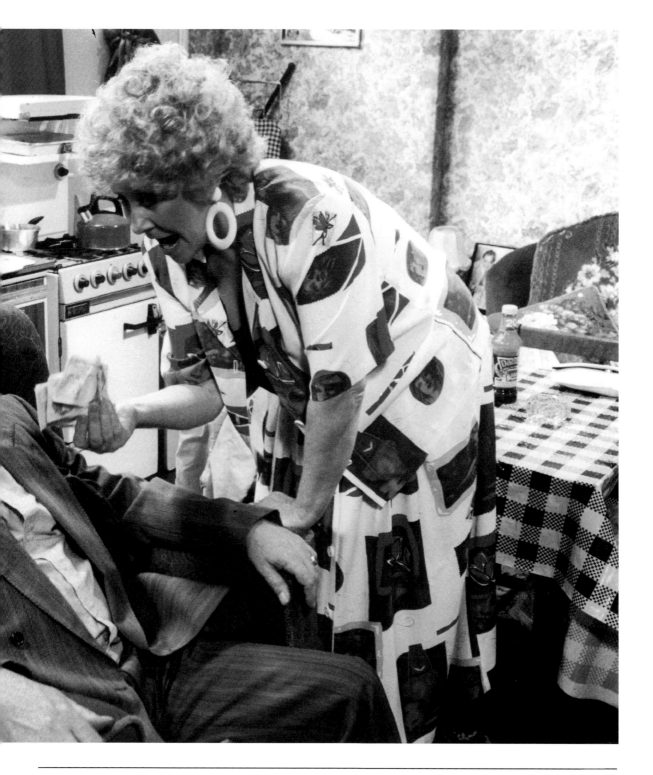

I knew I shouldn't have suggested a wet T-shirt contest.

bloke into the gents and – talking about getting to the bottom of it – the bloke gets the wrong idea about what I'm after and gives me a rare old belting.

All down to my lady wife. Again. Well you get fed up of it.

I wouldn't care but I got my first glimpse of how diabolical women can be when I was still only a kid, about sixteen I'd be, and I knew no better.

There was this girl round our way, Brenda Parkin, and she was famous for it. Red hot she was. A right little strumpet. Posh family and all – well, posh for round our way. Her dad was the local coal merchant. Anyway Brenda fancied me. She was only the coal merchant's daughter but she knew where to get a supply of best nuts. — *As if! All she'd get raw would be a handful of slack. – Vera*

Well this night, late on, I bumped into Brenda in the poshest chip shop in town. (It was the only chip shop round our way where they didn't have the salt and vinegar pots fastened to a length of chain.)

One thing leads to another, the vinegar fumes are intoxicating, and she takes me back to their house – says her mum and dad are away. This is good news because old man Parkin – and I'm not saying he was rougher than a bear's arse, but he sure as hell wasn't any smoother – he's famous for belting lads who come sniffing after Brenda.

So we go in the house, into her bedroom, and we're just getting going when there's a banging on the wall of the next bedroom. And I suddenly hear old Parkin's voice shouting, "Brenda! Who've you got in there with you?"

Brenda starts laughing. I start quivering, and next thing old Parkin's rushing in waving a nasty great poker about. I'm trapped. I grab my keks, rush to the window, scramble out on to the window ledge – and there's nowt else for it. I leap out into the night.

Well, thank God they lived in a bungalow, that's all I can say.

And there's a lesson for us all here. When you're playing away find out where the bird lives. And if it's one of these here tower blocks, forget it.

Dulcie Froggitt! She was another. At the time I met Dulcie I was running my own external glazing service business. And I'm up my ladder servicing her upstairs windows and Dulcie comes out wanting to know if I need my shammy wringing out at all.

Gutter journalism wrecks lives – Vera reads all about me and Dulcie in the local paper.

Dulcie Froggitt offering to wring out my shammy.

It turns out her old man's away working on an oil rig. And with Dulcie being lonely and me being kind-hearted before long I'm keeping the home fires burning and so forth.

I was very good to that woman. Sometimes I didn't even charge her for the windows, or not the full price anyway.

But she had this man-damaging streak. One afternoon she plied me with drink – desperate to get her way with me I suppose, well I can understand that – and the upshot is she gets me a bit wobbly and I fall off my ladder and break my ankle. A hospital job.

You'd think that would be enough pain and suffering to put a bloke through wouldn't you? Oh no. A couple of years later her husband, back off the rigs, walks into the Rovers looking for me and give a walloping.

And he'd no reason to do that. Because I HAD BY THIS TIME KICKED DULCIE INTO TOUCH.

That's how some women are. They complain to their husband that the boyfriend has gone off them. I call that diabolical.

Look at that Denise Osbourne. I gave her the old Duckworth charm and chat a couple of times, as much to keep my hand in as anything. She falls for me – I don't blame her for that – and invites me for a bit of hanky panky in her flat over the hairdressing salon.

I turn up as arranged (I had a bath and everything, though I didn't really need one). She lets me in the shop and leads me up the stairs to the flat.

And then on the landing she stops and puts this kinky proposition. She only wants me to get my clothes off on the landing – while she goes inside the flat – and then rush in to her in the nuddy.

Well that's disgusting isn't it? So I said – fine. Start getting my gear off, only she stops me, says she's changed her mind. Opens the flat door, leads me in – and VERA IS SITTING THERE WITH A GLASS IN HER HAND, NOT JUST VERA BUT HALF THE FLAMING STREET!

This is Denise Osbourne's idea of fun, teasing me. I tell you, I sometimes get like a vision of rushing into that flat with no clothes on, and there's Vera and the neighbours … I go all cold and shuddery just thinking about it. Women like her shouldn't be let out.

There have been times in my life when I've been bashed AND I HAVEN'T EVEN DONE ANYTHING.

This is what rankles. I have been bashed in mistake for my brother Cliff. I have been bashed by men who mistook me for their wife's boyfriend. Wrongly. That is the unfair part.

What it all amounts to is this. Some women, dangerous women, want to get men fighting over them. They lead a bloke on and then tell their husbands this bloke is after them. They are trying to make their husbands jealous so that they will show their passion BY BASHING ME.

Or you.

What can the sophisticated man about town do to ward this off? Here, culled from years of painful experience, are a few tips.

Beware of the woman who carries a big handbag. In my experience – big handbag, big husband.

Watch yourself with any bird who wears a gold cross on a chain round her neck. These tend to be randy birds – fine so far I agree. They also tend to be holy rollers. And in my experience religious women who are also nymphomaniacs make a bad combination.

One way or another you end up on your knees. And if you are only praying you'll be lucky.

Women who keep moaning about their husbands. These are bad news in my experience. The more they go on about him, the more likely you are ending up as a pillock whose function is to get a broken nose while revitalising their marriage.

Keep a sharp eye and ear for the way a woman carries on in pubs. In particular listen out for any of the following remarks, all of which have led to nasty moments for yours truly:

"Jack, that bloke's pushing in front. You were here before him."

"Jack, while you were in the gents this bloke insulted me."

"You're not going to let him get away with that are you Jack?"

Clock any of these, or similar, and you will do well to head for home and see if there is anything worth watching on the telly. If you don't – you will spend a lot of your life in casualty departments.

There are more and more of these dangerous women about. No wonder sperm counts are falling. No wonder decent fun-loving blokes like me are getting so bewildered you sometimes see us trying to sit down on our elbows.

My Friend Frank Sinatra

Talent is not something you can learn, it is something you are born with. Everyone has some talent and once you recognise where your true talent lies, you must be prepared to seize opportunities and make the most of your gift whether it be as a sportsman, a tradesman, a lover, an artiste or whatever.

I am fortunate enough to have been gifted with multifarious talents but if I should be thankful for any one particular talent then it is my glorious singing voice.

Since I took the Rovers Return on, I have had to put my singing career on hold, as we say in show-business. But even to this day, late at night when there are just a few favoured friends stood supping at the bar, I can be persuaded to do a rendition of a few great ballads once the <u>doors have been locked and I am in</u> the mellow mood. *So nobody can get out! – Vera*

I give them the numbers that are identified with me. Songs like "My Way" which I can say, in all honesty, I sing better than anybody.

Oh, yes. I can hear you scoffing. You are saying, "Come on! The all-time greats have sung that song." Course they have. But the way I sing it simply knocks everybody out. They don't want to hear anything else. They won't even let me do an encore. You see, when you've heard me sing "My Way", there is no way I or anybody else can top it.

The song is mine – who says so? Only the Guvnor. The Chairman Of The Board. Old Blue Eyes. Yes – Francis Albert Sinatra.

Life is a mysterious thing. I have already mentioned that my dear old father had no ear for music. Although he had a powerful voice –

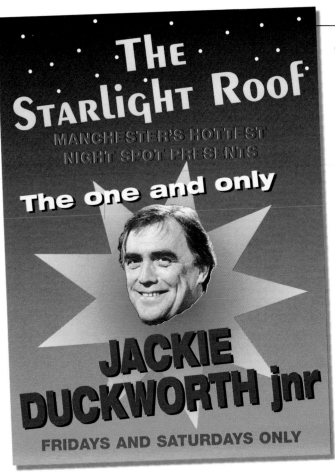

when he was out with he cart you could hear him shouting "Rag a bone!" five streets away – he did not have the precious gift of melody which I have been blessed with.

All right, all right I hear you say, but what's this got to do with Sinatra? OK, here it comes, and if I tell a word of a lie, may my manhood wither, may I be caught by Vera with my fingers in her handbag and may I be struck from behind by a sockful of wet cacky.

Like I said, coming to the end of the 1960s, I'd had my fill of groups. I'd gone solo and was doing the great standards – and a few little ballads I composed myself. There was one of mine I called "Unbeknownst (to me she fell in love with you)" which I swear I keep hearing in "Phantom Of The Opera". I'm not knocking young Andrew, good luck to the lad, all I'm saying is that you never know who is out there in the dark, part of that many headed monster we entertainers call the audience.

That was how I came to meet Frank and the opportunity presented itself for me to use my talents to take me onwards and upwards. Sadly, I did not take full advantage of the situation partly, perhaps, because I was so awestruck by the showbiz legend that is Frank Sinatra. I was booked to sing in this night spot where all the Manchester in-crowd went. The Starlight Roof it was called, in this basement just behind the town hall.

You got a sophisticated crowd in there. The tone was dead cosmopolitan. The bloke who ran it, Belgian Sid, was a real trendsetter in Manchester. I think it is fair to say that he created the fashion for Hush Puppies around there. Great sense of humour, too – a great practical joker. He loved setting fire to people's trousers. As soon as you walked in you could sniff the sophisticated ambulance of the place because in the lobby there was this mynah bird, black as your hat it was, which used to sit on a little perch and sidle up to you and say, "I'm a turkey."

So anyway, on this particular night, the old tonsils were working well and I finished the act as usual with my tribute to Frank. I went through the card. "All The Way," "Strangers In The Night," "Something Stupid" (which I always dedicated to Vera) and the big finish, "My Way". I had that audience spellbound. During my act there was not one single fight, which speaks for itself.

I was in my dressing room after (I'll never forget that dressing room. Belgian Sid had put a sign up above the urinal – "Please Do Not Drop Fag Ends In The Trough As It Makes Them Soggy And Difficult To Light"). When Sid himself walks in and says, "Jack, who do you think we've got in the club tonight? Only Frank Sinatra! And he wants to meet you!"

Of course, I thought he was pulling my plonker, but he swore blind he wasn't. So then I thought it must be some bloke pretending to be Sinatra. But Sid said, "Look, he says if you don't come and say hello, he's going to send his pals in here to break your legs."

Then I knew it must be him.

What a moment that was. At the best table in the house, the one with the four good legs, sat Frank Sinatra. He was smaller than he looks on screen – but then they all are, aren't they? Somebody was telling me that Sean Connery's only four foot three. Frank was wearing sunglasses, even though it was darker than the inside of a coalman's trousers in the club to start with.

There was another bloke with him – turned out to be some kind of film director – and two big tough minders. "Jack, my friend," says Frank, "I just want to tell you fella – you are the greatest. What are you drinking? I'll have whatever you're having, and so will the boys. You were terrific, fella. From now on I am going to sing "My Way" your way. If you are not the finest singer in the land, I will plait sawdust."

This was fantastic, coming from the Guvnor. "Thank you, Frank," I said, trying to stay humble. "Do not mind me saying this, but, you know, just then you sounded a bit Lancashire."

The bloke with him, the film director, piped up. "Mr Duckworth," he said, "this is in strict confidence, but Frank is in this neck of the woods researching and getting dialogue coaching for a motion picture. What we call in Hollywood a biopic. The George Formby Story.

Like a lot of these film projects, it never got made. These things happen in showbusiness. By now, though, they had set my mind at rest and if I had any doubts about it being Frank, they were swept away ten minutes later because he told me things about Ava Gardner that only he could have known – if you take my meaning. I told him some things about Vera, though I have to admit he didn't seem that interested.

The longer we sat there supping ale and chatting the better his Lancashire accent got. That's talent, you see. A little bit of practice and he was damn near perfect. Then Frank and the film director went into a huddle and they kept looking at me, weighing me up like, and finally Frank says, "Jackie, baby, I am going to make a picture here in your country called *The Naked Runner*. How would you like to be in it as my stunt double?"

They explained that in the film Frank would have to run round a night-club with no clothes on. In the nuddy. Only it would be me, not Frank, who

Me and Frank leaving the Starlight Roof.

did this bit. They said they could do the test right now, it was up to me This is how things are in showbiz.

So I took my kit off and did a streak round the club. The place went wild and at the end I got a big hand. I'm not sure whose, but if the lady whose hand it was reads this I would like her to get in touch for the sake of old times.

Frank and this film director had another huddle while I was getting my keks back on and then the director took me aside. "Jack," he says, "you did great. You are bigger made than Frank, but that is OK. You are definitely in the running for the part. It is between you and Sir Ralph Richardson."

I never heard any further, so this Richardson bloke must have got the nod. But, like I keep saying, that is showbiz.

Well, Frank had to leave after that, but he took me by the hand and said, "Jackie, baby, if you came stateside, if you came to Vegas, you could be huge. You could be one of my prat pack."

"Prat pack?" says I. "I thought it was the rat pack."

"We would change it in your honour," says Frank. Then he was off into the night. What a night that was. I'll never forget it. Engraved on my heart that night is . . . first of the fourth, 1969.

Course I never did go out there to Las Vegas. Well, you've got to be Italian, haven't you? But making the most of my God given talent – and I'm not just talking about the singing here – almost landed me a big time singing deal and a movie contract to boot.

Whatever your own particular talents are – and everybody's good at something – make the most of them.

Publicity shot given to me by Frank Sinatra for the film that he never made – The George Formby Story..

Man's Best Friend

Forget all that rubbish about dogs. Man's best friend is his motor car, his passion wagon. Without wheels a man turns into a stop-at-home. With what I've got at home can you think of anything worse? And for a young man a sound rule to follow is – never let a day go by without some by-play in a lay-by.

As for these politicians and friends of the planet and such like, the ones who keep saying we must get shut of our cars and use public transport instead – well I think that's disgusting.

You don't want that kind of thing on the bus do you?

It has always baffled me when people say the motor car is a sex thimble. I mean, you want a thimble when there's a possibility of getting your finger pricked.

You want a motor car when there's the possibility of it being the other way about.

But then again they always say a motor car should tell you something about the nature of the bloke who's driving it. Well by rights I ought to be behind the wheel of a big powerful Jaguar.

From the day I started noticing girls I knew I needed my own transport. I started with a hoop and a stick. And then I had a bald car tyre that my dear old father give me for Christmas one year when I was about seven. I used to bowl it round the streets and before New Year's Day I'd run over two cats and a policeman's foot.

So it was a great day for me – and the local birds – when I got my first proper car. A Ford Popular it was, one careful previous owner, shame about the other four, with leopard-skin seat covers.

It was dead classy. And there must have been summat inspiring about them leopard skin seat covers – brought out the animal in me I daresay – because in that car I was pulling birds like there was no tomorrow. The luckiest car I ever had. And when the time come to sell it and I was doing a 'for sale' sign to pop on the dashboard I could write on that sign WITH COMPLETE HONESTY – 'plenty of poke'.

Even though I was thinking more of the car's history than its acceleration.

Now the luckiest car Vera ever had, she only had because I won it for her. That woman's had a charmed life, ever since she got me in her clutches. This magazine she reads you see, *Woman's Choice* it's called, full of the usual rubbish, ten ways to drive your husband wild – she doesn't need any hints on that, she can do it already.

Anyway, they had this contest one time to win a car, Vauxhall Nova it was. What it was, the readers had to write in with a snappy slogan saying why their husband was 'husband of the year'.

give over. The only car that would tell you summat about our Jack would be a little red mini with two flat tyres!

– Vera

Try as I might, I just couldn't shake her off.

My old Ford Pop. Plenty of poke, but in the back seat, not under the bonnet!

So I went in for this competition. Anyway I also figured out it would have to be a woman's name on the entry form – some blokes wouldn't have sussed that would they? – so I sent it in under Vera's name.

And like I say I won the car. Because I come up with a brilliant slogan. "My husband is husband of the year because – right from the day we were married he has made my life one long honeymoon."

The lying toad. 'one long Honeymoon'. There's been nothing long about living with him, that's his trouble! – Vera

Vera could not have thought up anything as clever as that, not in a million years. But you know what she did? I still go cold when I think of it.

She claimed the car belonged to her.

She would not even let me drive it.

Well that's what she thought.

Boxing clever as usual, I got the keys out of her handbag while she was snoring in front of the telly one night and got copies cut.

So that's how he did it. Right. And I do not snore.

After that, I used to borrow the car when she was at work and had many a happy afternoon in it, especially with a lady friend of mine who shall be nameless only her initials are Dulcie Froggitt.

A TART – Go with anybody for a bag of chips! – Vera

I've driven all sorts in my time. Drove a tipper lorry for the council for a couple of years. In my experience it was no good for pulling birds. Not the really classy ones anyway.

And for a few years I was a cabbie. Happy days and nights they were, because driving a taxi is a great way of meeting women, and some of my greatest triumphs with the opposite thingy occurred in that manner.

When you are driving a cab you tend to come across what we in the profession call 'bitter birds'. Don't get me wrong. They don't drink pints (always a bad sign), although they do tend to ring for a cab from pubs and clubs a fair bit.

These are birds who have had a nasty experience. They've been abandoned in the bar by some shifty boyfriend. Or they've just had cross words with the old man and decided to leave him to his ale.

So they have a sorrowful tale to tell, you see, about man's inhumanity to women. For a bloke like myself who can manage not to crack out laughing as they rabbit on, and do a sympathetic murmur from time to time as we drive along – well, let's just say I often got very very friendly with some of my lady passengers.

Especially such as might discover that she hadn't enough cash in her handbag to pay the fare.

But cabbing is not all gravy. I hate to say this, but there is a bad side to human nature and …

Vera snatches the keys, but the car were rightly mine.

some women cannot be trusted.

There are some totally immoral women knocking about these days. They say things like, "Wait here while I get the money for you." What has happened to human decency in this country?

And then there was one monster in female form who, when we were parked and getting friendly, suggested it would be easier for me to get my keks off if I got out of the car.

When I did she got behind the wheel and drove off. Laughing.

Practical hint: in this situation the man of the world puts the ignition key in his trousers' pocket. Simple when you know, but easy to overlook. I wish there had been some experienced bloke to give me these helpful tips that I am giving you.

I would probably be cabbing to this day if it had not been for a stupid woman called – you guessed it – Vera Duckworth.

Her and Ivy used to go to bingo a lot. Course poor old Ivy's gone to the great leisure centre in the sky now. But at that time they were bingo mad, and one night they had a good win, couple of hundred quid.

Dulcie and I Christening the back seat of the car I won.

I gave our Terry our old car at a very fair price. The swine still owes me for it.

So then they had me driving them round all the pubs while they celebrated. And I couldn't just sit there in the cab while they were supping could I?

And so it was all Vera's fault. I got breathalysed and lost my licence for twelve months. And that was the end of cabbing.

And for the next twelve months till I got my licence back, Vera had to do what, come to think of it, she's been doing ever since I met her. Drive me to drink.

Still. I'd sooner have the Rovers than be a cabbie. So it's come out okay really. And I've still got a car. Funny, I hadn't thought about it till just this minute ... I've not had any fun in this car. It's not that I'm getting past it or anything, it's just that I haven't got round to it yet. I will. Don't you worry. There'll be a few more notches on the old fan belt before I've finished. *It's pathetic really, at his age.*

Fred Elliott, the local butcher, sold me this present car. He's all right is Fred, bit rough, not got my polish. But *Vera* he's all right. In his own way. And he's going to get me into the Square Dealers before so long, you know, the funny handshake lads, you know, nudge nudge, you be right with me and I'll be right with you.

I don't blame Fred really. Not his fault the car's a bit of, well, it's temperamental. Supposed to be a Sierra, I think it's more of a cross with a Fiesta ... sort of a Siesta. Come off the day shift at Halewood I daresay.

I test drove a Merc not long back. They're all right and I could have one, no problem. If I wanted. Just like that.

But you'd be a fool to yourself having a Merc round Coronation Street wouldn't you? You what? Park a Merc on the Street round our way? You wouldn't chuckle. The kids'd have it away.

No, I'm better off with something a bit battered, nobody's idea of a joy ride.

Now we're back to flaming Vera again.

Abroad

Sooner or later – women being what they are – the wife or girlfriend is going to turn all sulky and awkward and start pestering you to take her on a foreign holiday.

It happens to us all. I remember the day it happened to me. Vera had been dead quiet and broody all day. I thought she must have noticed her purse was light.

But no. All of a sudden she bursts out. "How come everybody else goes abroad for their holidays?" she says, looking hard-done-to. "All the girls at work have been. I'm sick to death of it. And if they can go flying off to foreign parts, why can't we?"

I give her one of my best big wide beaming smiles. (It makes my ears move up the side of my head a bit, and then my specs slide down my nose a touch. A lot of women have told me it has a dead sexy effect.)

"Vera love," I said. "You fancy a foreign holiday? That's fine with me."

It seemed to surprise her. She said, "You mean you'll go along with it? We can go abroad somewhere for us holidays?"

Practising for going abroad in Blackpool.

"Vera my little stocking top," I said, "if that is what you want – that is what you shall have. If you find the money – leave the rest to me."

You see, it's good for women to have something to save up for. And the way I look at it, it's comforting to know that somewhere about the house there's another biscuit tin with a little fund in it, just waiting to be tracked down if you get an emergency or a good tip on the three-thirty at Haydock.

Some people get frightened about the flying. I know this for A FACT. The couple of times we've flown I have seen people sick, actually sick, with fear.

Well it is not fear I have been sick from. Because I get well stuck into the ale before we get on the plane. Some blokes tell me they can't fancy supping five or six pints of beer at 7 o'clock in the morning. But that is what airport bars are for. And, as I tell these people, you have to put your mind to it, you have to force yourself.

The way I look at it, being a bit of a philosopher on the quiet, when the grim reaper comes for you with his scythe – it is no good ducking. And if

Not a holiday abroad. Not abroad and not much of a holiday, neither.

our plane is going to land sooner than it is supposed to with a nasty bang, I don't want to know anything about it.

So I bevvy up beforehand, and then as soon as we get aboard I show the nearest air hostess my doctor's note.

I got this note off the doctor a few years back, when I happened to be down at the surgery having my bad back looked at. (He claimed he couldn't find anything wrong incidentally. But is it my fault he's not much good at his job?)

One of them old dragons they call receptionists called him into the corridor about something, so quick as a flash I ripped the top page off his personalised note pad. And when I got back home I wrote myself a really good doctor's note.

'To whom it may concern – on medical grounds my patient Mr Jack Duckworth is strongly advised to get as much alcohol down him as he can manage. He should be given every assistance. In view of his condition he is not to be opposed in any way." Signed with a big squiggle.

So anyway I always show this note to people like air hostesses. They seem to understand that I need a good flow of drink to steady myself. And by the end of the flight I am so steady I can hardly move at all.

Nice girls, mostly, those air hostesses. And they definitely go for me. I always get a smile. There was one who smiled that much I thought I was in with a chance of joining the mile-high club. So I kept lurking about near the toilets at the back of the plane, just on the off chance. Only she didn't seem to get a chance to come down that end and in the finish I got a funny look off a bloke with an earring.

We had our portraits done on holiday in Spain.

Another good reason for supping plenty on the plane – it gives you resistance against foreign germs. They tell you not to drink the water don't they? Mind you, it doesn't apply to me, that. Because I don't even drink water when I'm at home.

Yes, they're mostly nice the air hostesses. But the first time we went, going back a bit now, there was one who drove me spare. She handed these forms out and said foreigners had to fill them in before they could get off at the other end.

By 'foreigners' she meant us! Is that barmy or is that barmy?

Well I filled the form up anyway, but then she comes bustling back. "Excuse me, Mr Duckworth," she says, "but here where it says 'Where born' you have put 'at home'."

"That's correct", I says.

"No, but what it is," she says, "they want more precise detail than that."

So I crossed out "at home and put "back bedroom" instead. And even then she wasn't satisfied.

Once you get into this going abroad game there is no doubt about the best place to go. Spain. I know this for definite, because we have been twice.

The beauty of it is, in Spain you don't get much foreign aggravation. You can get proper British ale. You can get egg and chips so you don't have to eat a lot of mucked-about foreign food. And there are so many people on holiday from the dear old U of K, you don't even have to meet any foreigners.

Not that I've owt against foreigners. I like everybody me, unless and until they give me a hard time. Now some people grumble about the Jerries. They say they're always nipping down to the swimming pool at cock shout to put towels on the deck chairs.

Well that's no bother. What you do, when you want a deck chair by the pool, you just chuck the towels in the water and sit yourself down.

All right, sooner or later some German bloke will come grumbling at you about – "this is mein chair and where is mein towel?

All you have to do is give him a wink and say, "Fritz, mine friend, where we come from we have a saying – bums keep seats." You probably won't even have to mention the war.

By the way, people tell you the thing to do is learn a bit of the lingo before you go.

Forget it. I learned this the hard way when I was doing my Army service abroad. In Wales this was. Not far from Rhyl.

I was young and idealistic then. Brotherhood of man. (Whatever happened to them?) All that stuff. When I was out of barracks I used to nip off to some local pub, and if I met a local I'd give him – or her, yes, or her – a big hello. Nothing. No response. It used to get me down I tell you.

More flesh on display than Fred Elliot's butcher shop window.

Then the landlord in this pub I used to go in said, "They're not being funny with you. They don't understand you. Speak to them in Welsh! Say Yacky Dar. It means howdo."

OK, next night I get out of barracks, head for the pub, and I see this bloke cycling towards me. So when he gets level I say, "Yacky Dar."

And the bloke on the bike says, "Buzz off you Welsh git."

It sours you, that sort of thing.

So don't bother learning Spanish or any other lingo. You can always communicate if you speak clearly and give them helpful gestures.

The word "bastardo" is widely understood abroad, in my experience. Also the phrase "Hey Abdul! Where is our pudding?" seems to get across. Also "Encore the vino!"

Olympics Day was a holiday – and these eggs were my breakfast!

The Spanish themselves are a wonderful warm-hearted people. And very hospitable to strangers. I know this for a fact because on our first ever trip, our first night out there in Benidorm, me and Vera were out on the town, doing a tour of the bars, and we got separated.

Now answer me this – if a Spaniard got lost over here in England, and couldn't remember which hotel he was staying at, and met some British soldiers out on the bevvy, would he get friendly treatment? Would he be given plenty to drink and told to keep his money in his pocket? Would he be taken back to barracks and smuggled in and found a bed for the night?

I don't think so. But this is what happened to Vera when we were in Benidorm.

I call that real hospitality. And when Vera did manage to get back to our hotel next morning she told me those lads could not do enough for her.

You do get the odd Spaniard who lets the side down. Their coppers wear really daft hats. This is not just my opinion, this is A FACT. And when you are having a few drinks in a bar and a policeman walks in wearing a really daft hat, you are entitled to have a bit of fun aren't you? It is coming to something when you cannot laugh at a policeman's hat.

But despite police brutality I left that bar with my head held high.

Vera held my head and this very nice bloke from Bradford held my feet.

One last pointer. There is a snag to going abroad for your holiday. Well, there is if you live round Coronation Street.

It is a pound to a pinch of snuff that the day you get home you will bump into Percy Sugden who, quick as a flash, will give you the traditional Lancashire welcome back.

"Hello," says Percy. "You're not very brown. Have you not had nice weather? It's been lovely here."

*I'm saying nothing
– Vera.*

What's it All About

I woke up in the middle of the night just recently. Curtains were open. Moonlight was coming in, illuminating Vera's face as she lay there, like some abandoned vehicle under a tarpaulin, fast akip, snoring her head off.

The curlers were glinting in the moonbeams, the face was covered in some gunk she swears by. I wouldn't care but it doesn't actually hide anything, it just gives her a layer of grease.

There was me, studying her. And I couldn't help thinking to myself -

Why are we here?
What are we put on this earth for?
Is it some kind of initiative test?

Vera reckons we have a lot of lives. She claims we come back as somebody or something different — depending on how we behave ourselves in the present existence.

Well, if that is the case, I can only say I must have done something really terrible last time I was here, to get Vera bunged on to me. Next time I ought to be due for something dead cushy.

Now according to Vera – I don't listen all that much, you'd go dolally if you paid too much attention – she's been this, she's been that. Lady-in-waiting at court in the olden days, Egyptian slave girl, and one time she was a princess.

In my opinion she must have been an Austin Princess, because her face does put you in mind of the boot end of that particular model.

If there is anything in this claim of our Vera's I would not mind coming back as a pigeon, me. All right, the cats are always after you. And the odd hawk. But apart from that it's not a bad life.

First thing I would do is swoop low over Vera, tweeting, "Here's mud in your eye" or tweets to that effect.

But knowing my luck, even if there is something in this reincarnation theory, I will come back as a tin of milk.

Don Brennan explains why Magnus Magnusson is not as smart as he thinks he is.

Still, it makes you think. Late at night there is often a lot of deep talk in the Rovers bar, and somebody will say, "Why are we here?"

To which some cynical bastard replies, "Because it's Newton and Ridley's ale. Get 'em in."

But the question still nags you. My pal Don Brennan, the taxi driver, he had that Magnus Magnusson in the back of the cab once.

"Magnus," he said – he's matey to everybody is Don – "Magnus," he said, "you're a clever feller. What is it all about, eh?"

And do you know? Magnus Magnusson COULD NOT TELL HIM. Which just goes to show, these brainy types have no more idea than the rest of us.

And then again, all these different religions. What you are, it just depends which house, mud hut, tent or igloo you happen to turn up in.

My pal Harvey Nuttall, who runs Nuttall's brewery and is a really deep thinker, he says it all comes down to a song or chant he was taught as a lad –

> Roses are reddish
> Violets are bluish
> It if wasn't for Christmas
> We'd all be Jewish.

And you have to admit, there is something in this.

Vera

When you're a pub landlord you're always getting asked for advice. One of my regulars the other night – well I could tell something was on his mind because he was buying his own ale.

"Jack," he said in the finish, "I think the lodger's at it with the missus. Only I could be wrong, so I don't want to tackle him about it, because he's not a bad bloke and anyway, he's company for my whippet."

Delicate, you see. So I had a think, and then give my advice. "Put his rent up," I said, "and if he doesn't grumble – you'd best have a sharp word with the missus. Only not in front of the whippet because they're highly strung."

Well, naturally, the bloke was grateful for my advice. And so I had a pint with him, and he said, "Jack lad – what would YOU do if you were in

Our Vera was definitely in need of a few improvements.

that position. If Vera was at it with some bloke, what would you do?"

Quick as a flash I said, "I would go round to this bloke's house. And I would break his white stick across my knee and stuff the pieces up his jumper."

So we all had a good laugh. Except Vera. She hasn't got much sense of humour.

The amazing thing is though, there are SOME MEN WHO FANCY VERA.

It is hard to believe but there you are. What they go for, I do not know. She keeps telling me she's got some attractive features, for instance she's always claiming she's got beautifully sculpted cheekbones.

I just wish myself they were the facial kind of cheek bones, but there you go.

But to be fair, sometimes we get a customer in the Rovers who sups a drop too much of Nuttall's Midnight Special – puts a refill in anybody's ballpoint that does – and then starts chatting Vera up across the bar.

I have to step in then. Mind you, I know what they're really after is a free pint. And any woman who has the power to put a free drink in your hand is, let's face it, an attractive woman.

Vera with the Pratt.

There was just one bloke who was different. Chap called Lester Fontayne.

That wasn't his real name mind you. I heard his real name was Pratt, which would make a lot of sense. Fontayne was his stage name, you see, he played the piano in a bar we used to go in at a holiday camp in North Wales.

And he was DEFINITELY AT IT WITH VERA. Late one night in the snooker room. A proper competition sized table and all. I call that disgusting. I know for a fact the cloth got ripped.

He'd have been snookered all right, if I'd caught him. I'd have cleared the balls off that table faster than Hurricane Higgins.

Course, Vera tried to crack on it was all in my imagination. But a couple of years after this she had a few days holiday in Blackpool without me. But SHE WAS NOT ON HER OWN. No, she met flaming Lester Fontayne again.

I only found out about this because one day I came across a photo of the two of them together. She had hidden it, but luckily I stumbled across it quite by chance. It was in her handbag.

Yeah, he was different. For a start he was nice to me!
— Vera

I give her some stick over that! A right tongue-lashing. I played steam. She tried to crack on she was just getting her own back because I happened to have played away a time or two.

I wasn't having that! She knows damn well it's different for men. We can't help putting ourselves about a bit. Mother Nature MAKES US DO THAT. As I have said before, it is all in our jeans.

That's what he thinks. – Vera

I think she's learned her lesson. And I will say this, it is the only time she has strayed.

You might wonder why I give a stuff about what Vera might get up to with somebody else. I wonder myself. It's not easy to explain.

But a pal of mine was in hospital not long back, for a major operation – having this tattoo removed. And before you say having a tattoo removed is not a major operation – it is when what you're having removed is the name 'Peggy Sue Winterbottom' starting up between the shoulder-blades and finishing fairly close to where the sun don't shine.

Anyroad, he had this wart you see. And the bloke in the white coat said to him, do you want us to take your wart off while we're at it? He decided to keep the wart. Like he said, he'd lived with it a long time, he'd sort of got attached to it.

Well.....that's how I feel about Vera.

Aw, in't he lovely! I know I go on about him, but I mean, deep down he really cares. I think this is the nicest thing he's ever said about me. Ooh wait till I get him in bed tonight. – Vera

Regrets

Regrets? Yes, I have had a few. But then again, too few to mention. Hang on. Now I come to think of it there do happen to be a few that I wouldn't mind getting off my chest. This palmist on Blackpool front studied my hand one time and said to me: "I can see you have a lot of trouble in your life – all through being too nice to people." Well, that is dead right.

I was too nice to Tina Fowler when she was barmaid at the Rovers in Bet Gilroy's day. I wined and dined her at great expense and then she refused to join me in the back seat of the motor on the grounds that I was a married man!

I call that immoral, me. Especially in this day and age where there are people who never get chance of a good feed and a few bevvies.

Another regret that rankles with me. I have never been invited to a wife-swapping party. And I know why. They've seen Vera, haven't they?

I regret never having come face to face with the twisted bastard who invented the heavy-duty double gusset, a knicker knackerer if ever there was one. It would have give me great pleasure to offer the sadistic swine a knuckle sandwich.

Ditto the twerp who invented tights. I am a stocking-top man and always have been.

Similar to the trouble-making cow on Vera's magazine *Woman's Choice*. She keeps writing stuff like "Ten Ways To Turn Your Husband On" and "The Sex Olympics: Make Your Man A Bedroom Athlete". When this kind of porn is fed to a stupid and dangerously strong woman it can seriously affect a man's health.

One last thing. I wish my dear old father could have lived to see me master of my own pub. He would have been proud. Pissed too, of course. But proud.

I also regret Vera's mother did not live to see me with my own pub.

Aw, you see, he can be dead nice when he want.

Because it would have given me great pleasure to inform the old cow she was barred from the premises.

I take that back. And so will he when I have finished with him!! — Vera